10 lessons from the future

10 lessons from the future

Tomorrow is a matter of choice.
Make it yours

Wolfgang Grulke

FT Prentice Hall
FINANCIAL TIMES

An imprint of Pearson Education

London · New York · San Francisco · Toronto · Sydney
Tokyo · Singapore · Hong Kong · Cape Town · Madrid
Paris · Milan · Munich · Amsterdam

PEARSON EDUCATION LIMITED

Head Office:
Edinburgh Gate
Harlow CM20 2JE
Tel: +44 (0)1279 623623
Fax: +44 (0)1279 431059

www.pearsoned.co.uk

First published in South Africa by @One Communications 2000
This edition first published in Great Britain in 2001
First ARP Impression 98

ISBN-13: 978-0-273-65329-5

British Library Cataloguing in Publication Data
A CIP catalogue record for this book can be obtained from the British Library

ARP Impression 98

Designed by Claire Brodmann Book Designs, Burton on Trent
Typeset by Pantek Arts Ltd, Maidstone, Kent

Printed in Great Britain by Clays Ltd, St Ives plc

To my daughter **Victoria**

You inspired me to leave a mark on the future.
May you gain the wisdom
to choose your ideal future and
thrive in it happily.

Contents

Foreword

The 20th century bore witness to some of the most dramatic changes humanity has ever undergone. The automobile changed the world; the airplane made it possible to have breakfast in Paris and lunch in New York City; radio and television delivered news and entertainment from all parts of the globe in real time. Nuclear energy was unleashed for both good and evil.

But the changes brought about by the Internet may turn out to be the most dramatic of them all.

The Internet has collapsed time and distance, forever changing the way we live, learn, work and play. We are rapidly approaching the point where we can have anything, anytime, anyplace.

Individuals now have more power and influence than ever before. The opportunities are endless, and we have only just scratched the surface. The question which has to be answered, and it can only be answered by you is: "Are you ready?"

Because if you aren't, you will miss out on one of the great adventures of the 21st century. The opportunity to be part of a truly global community.

I have had the pleasure of working with Wolfgang Grulke over many years. One of the attributes I most admire in him is his never-ending quest for knowledge. He has a highly inquisitive mind and the unique ability to understand complex phenomena. But more important, he understands how to translate what is happening into pragmatics.

Ten Lessons from the Future is an excellent example of his unique ability in action. There are valuable lessons to be learned from reading this book, and they can be applied to one's life as well as one's business. If you don't take the time to read this book, you will truly be missing the opportunity to get "Net Ready."

John Sifonis
Director, Internet Business Solutions Group
Cisco Systems

John is the author of *Dynamic Planning: The Art of Managing Beyond Tomorrow* (1994), *Corporation on a Tightrope* (1996) and *Net Ready: Strategies for Success in the E-conomy* (1999).

Author's preface and acknowledgements

Forecasting is difficult, especially when it concerns the future. This phrase has stuck in my mind ever since I read it many years ago. I can't even remember where. It may have been a kind of intellectual graffiti that just drifted into my consciousness.

Many years of work in business strategy has convinced me that indeed, forecasting is folly. The more the world changes, the less appropriate it becomes to extrapolate from past successes. Somehow though, at a personal and business level, we have to think about the future and maximize our chances of thriving in it. The ability to contemplate the future appears to be one skill that differentiates humans from all other creatures on the planet.

More than ten years ago, in his superb book, *Future Perfect*, a Harvard Professor named Stan Davis articulated a radical new approach to the future. In essence, weaving together similar thoughts from many sources, he encouraged us to "plan backwards."

During many late nights working together, Stan and I discussed this approach. Imagine your ideal future in such detail that you can feel and touch it. Create a memory of the future to guide your every action today.

Create a powerful vision and a context for thousands of small actions, and subconsciously you will ratchet towards your desired destination, one small action at a time.

In practice, the discipline of planning backwards has a way of producing more rewarding results than you could achieve by simply extrapolating from today – it somehow bridges the "paradigm gap."

To me, Stan Davis's thinking resonated powerfully with the philosophies of another giant of strategic and systems thinking, Russell Ackoff. His words appeared to me as motherhood the first time I read them:

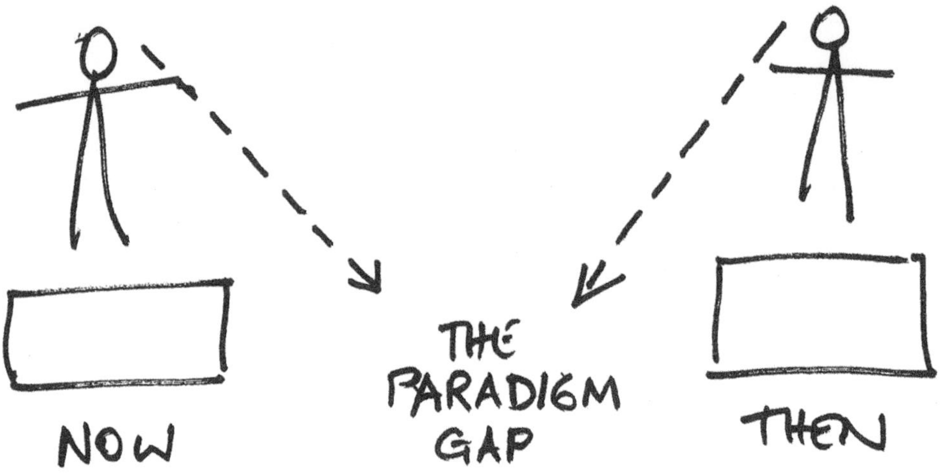
THE PARADIGM GAP
NOW
THEN

"With understanding, you can design and create your future."

Only much later did Ackoff's real wisdom become apparent to me. As traditional strategic planning and forecasting failed us, I learned to appreciate his insights at a totally practical level. Understand the future system that you will be a part of. Understand markets and customer needs the way they *will* be. Design your *idealized* role in this future context. Share it with those around you. Then you can *create* it!

Understand, design, create. Three simple but extremely powerful steps that have proven themselves increasingly useful in today's turbulent markets – for businesses, individuals and governments.

Let's look at the recent and often-cited example of the way the future was created in Apartheid-era South Africa. When you consider the diametrically opposing positions of the white minority government, and the leadership of such banned and exiled organizations as the African National Congress, it is astonishing that they could find anything to agree on, let alone negotiate a political settlement. Yet, during the early 1990s, these sworn enemies found a common set of goals, a common purpose, a sub-set of national possibilities that they could work towards.

In part, it's because they set out to plan scenarios, rather than attempt to forecast the future. In business or in politics, scenario-planning is a great way of building trust and avoiding the "It'll never happen here! Not in my lifetime!" reaction to radical views of the future. After all, you're just looking at scenarios. Alternative views.

Using alternative scenarios, the future literally becomes a matter of choice, not chance.

If you look back at the economic revolution of the past 30 years, you may find it hard to believe that the world was ever any different.

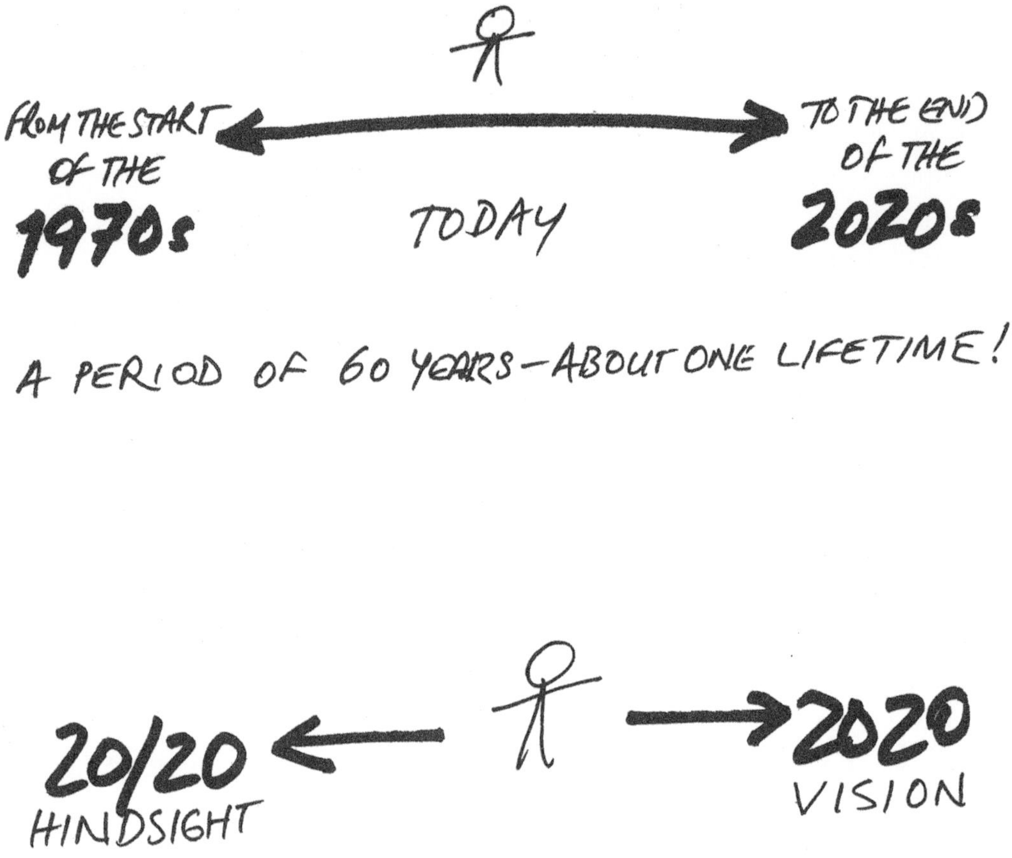
FROM THE START OF THE 1970s
TODAY
TO THE END OF THE 2020s
A PERIOD OF 60 YEARS—ABOUT ONE LIFETIME!
20/20 HINDSIGHT
2020 VISION

With hindsight we can see that the culture of the sixties and seventies spawned radical new attitudes, products and companies, all of which are taken for granted today.

But turn around and look at the future, and you find that most visions of the next 20 to 30 years sound like so much science fiction!

"Impossible," we say. "It just won't happen!"

Whatever happened to 20/20 vision?

The term "20/20 Vision" was coined in 1862 and is known as "The Snellen Fraction." It measures *normal* visual acuity at "optical infinity." It does not, as is popularly believed, represent *perfect* vision. Somehow our vision of 2020 and beyond seems profoundly stunted.

When we're faced with radical futures or radical technological forecasts, it's amazing how our minds cloud over. In their time, Dick Tracy's wrist phones were dismissed as sheer science fiction. Now, when we look at the amazing success of the cellphone over the past decade, it doesn't surprise us at all. We take the past technological revolutions completely in our stride.

With perfect 20/20 hindsight, nothing surprises us!

We look back to the late 1960s and are amazed that no-one forecast the radical success of television, the video recorder or the personal computer. Radical innovation and change just sneaked up on us. But of course today, thanks to perfect 20/20 hindsight, we know better – we could have predicted it all. Couldn't we?

My daughter Victoria put it succinctly: "You guys must have been really dumb not to see the personal computer coming!" With 20/20 hindsight, of course, she's absolutely right.

20/20 hindsight always works perfectly. 2020 vision is stunted, at best imperfect.

What we'll do in this book is look backwards, with perfect 20/20 hindsight, to the culture, technologies and business of the 1970s. We'll look at where we

1. UNDERSTAND!

↓

2. DESIGN!

↓

3. CREATE!

A DELIBERATE 3-STEP PROCESS
TO CHOOSE YOUR FUTURE

stand today, and we'll examine the rules of the game that will shape the future in the 2020s. Not specific technologies, no specific forecasts. Just a number of powerful trends that are emerging to shape our world. We'll examine the evidence we see all around us – in the culture of consumers, in exploding new technologies, in the radical new business models and in the behavior of governments and markets.

We'll be reminded that everything happens in cycles: products, fashion, our lives and, at a macro level, even economies. It was Christopher Meyer, who together with Stan Davis, inspired me to understand the changes enveloping us in terms of the economic cycles that form such a vital part of this book's introduction.

I hope that for *you,* the *Ten Lessons from the Future* will create a process of *understanding* that will help you *design* and *create* your own future. To help you *choose* your future from all possible futures waiting out there for you.

Today, as never before in the history of humanity, *you* have the power and the choice.

But *knowing,* alone, is never enough. You have to *do* something. A recent CNN advertising campaign proclaimed that "*You are what you know.*" I beg to differ. *You are what you do!*

Whatever you do as a result of reading this book, remember to turn Strategic *Thinking* into Strategic *Action.* Do something differently today that will shape your future tomorrow!

How to use this book

By its very nature, any book about the new world economy is a work-in-progress. It is organic, ever changing, never complete.

By the time you read this, much will have changed. Some things will have been proved right. Others may well have been proved wrong. Either way...

This book has been **designed**

to encourage you to read *actively*!

I am a passionate scribbler on large white spaces. When I communicate, I tend to communicate *actively,* creating images and pictures, spontaneously, at random, on walls, flip charts, or any other available surface.

Sometimes the page has been

intentionally left blank –

just for you

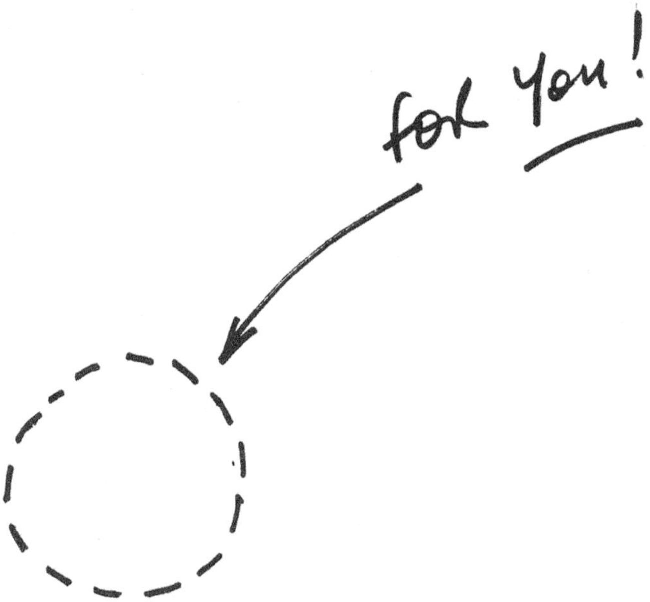

With that in mind, I have left the left-hand pages of this book essentially "blank." The future itself is a blank slate, waiting to be filled in by you and you alone. The blank pages in this book are a perfect metaphor for this way of thinking. Unable to resist the temptation, I've used some of the blank spaces to draw a few images of my own for you. I hope they'll illustrate the text in a more conceptual way. Sometimes my editor has taken the liberty of adding a quote from the text.

Sometimes the page has been intentionally left blank – just for you. Take a pen or pencil. Do it now. Add some graffiti yourself. Do some white-space thinking! Write down your expectations of this book and revisit them later. Air your views, if only to restate the ideas in the book, in ways more relevant to you or your business.

For you too, I hope this book will become your "work in progress."

Most of the books in my collection have margins covered in comments and sketches. I don't just read books. I actively interact with them! I encourage you to do the same with this book.

Finally, a few words of thanks.

To my editors, Gus Silber in South Africa and Richard Stagg at Pearson in London. To Gus, for his patience in following me and the FutureWorld Network of Gurus around the lecture circuit, innumerable interviews in the strangest of places and his creativity in translating many of my thoughts to paper. To Richard and his team for adding additional dimensions to an already challenging manuscript!

To my clients worldwide, our Network of Gurus and especially my dear friend Anton Musgrave – you taught me so much by allowing yourselves to be the laboratory of the New Economy, for radical untested ideas. You inspired me – and in the process you have become partners and close friends.

To my wife Terri – for giving me the stuff of dreams, universal magic and for changing my life beyond comprehension.

Wolfgang Grulke
The Universe
March 12, 2000

From all of me,

to all of you –

Enjoy!

1

Introduction

The silent revolution

> "You say you want a revolution...
>
> well, you know,
>
> we all want to change the world."

John Lennon, from the Beatles song, *Revolution*

Think about a revolution.

What do you see?

Workers and students rioting in the streets, banners flying high, statues toppling from their pedestals. In the age of CNN and the breaking story, we have grown accustomed to watching social and political upheaval as it happens.

In the safety of our living rooms and offices, we are transfixed by the staccato sound of gunfire, the heavy rhythm of sledgehammers against walls, the live-from-the-scene montages of distant cities ablaze.

Sooner or later, it all becomes part of the wallpaper, and we find ourselves slowly getting back to the business at hand, perhaps occasionally stealing a glance at the flickering tube in the corner of the room.

But the fact is, not every revolution is accompanied by scenes of violence. Not every revolution is transmitted in real-time, or hammered home by breathless reports from the battlefront.

Some **revolutions** arrive without fanfare.
Some revolutions take place **in silence.**
Some revolutions can turn **your life upside-down,**
without you even **being aware** that they are happening.

Let me give you a perfect example…

There is a revolution that is taking place all around you, right now, even as you hold this book in your hands.

It is a revolution that is as much a part of your life, as it is of mine. It is a revolution that is as natural, as all-encompassing, and as dynamic, as the revolution of the earth around the sun.

This is the **revolution** of you, me, and the person next door…
The Revolution of the **Empowered Individual!**

Never before, in the history of the world, have ordinary people held as much power, as much freedom, as much opportunity to accomplish extraordinary things. Never before have ordinary people been this much capable of changing the world, of seizing the future and making it happen.

How?

Firstly, by accepting and understanding that the world around us has already changed beyond recognition.

Gone are the limits, the boundaries, the time-zones that once kept us distant and apart from each other. Gone, in a very real sense, is the very notion of geographic distance and division.

In today's world – the world of networks and connections, the wide, wired world of the 24 × 7 × 52 economy – we truly are one, united, joined in destiny, irrespective of our personal politics, ideologies, or pinpoints on the planet.

In days gone by, in the age of the Industrial Economy, we instinctively sought to divide the world into the "haves" and the "have nots."

Today, in the age of the New Information Economy,
it would be more accurate to talk of **the "haves"**
and the **"want nots."**

MY EXPECTATIONS
of THIS BOOK

Because today, for the first time in history, anyone can claim access to the new global playing field, provided they play by the three golden rules:

- Be literate!
- Speak English!
- Get wired!

Today, whoever you are, whatever you do, wherever you live, work, and network, the choice is yours.

Today,
you hold the power in your hands.
Today, more than ever, the future belongs to you!
Just one question... are you ready for it?
Do you want it?

2

Economic turbulence

A clash of life cycles

"The last few years of the 20th century were the most volatile years in economic history. It's as if we were being buffeted by larger and larger waves of change, arriving faster and with greater force."

But the waves had been building up for centuries.

Five hundred years ago, the annual increase in personal incomes was no more than 0.1 percent. Over the past 50 years, that increase has grown to an average of around 3 percent a year.

One hundred years ago, capital flows worldwide were dominated by a few thousand wealthy families. Today they are in the hands of hundreds of millions of individual investors.

During the past 50 years, two major revolutions have transformed world markets and the world economy. The combination of open global markets and technology has created vast new deregulated markets, wired together by a converging information highway, and dominated by new and transformed organizations that are rewriting the rules of business.

Now, we have the distinct impression that an economic tsunami is coming. We sense the rumbling beyond the horizon. We hear of an e-commerce revolution that will create growth in excess of 75 percent per annum and engulf 20 percent of world GDP within five years.

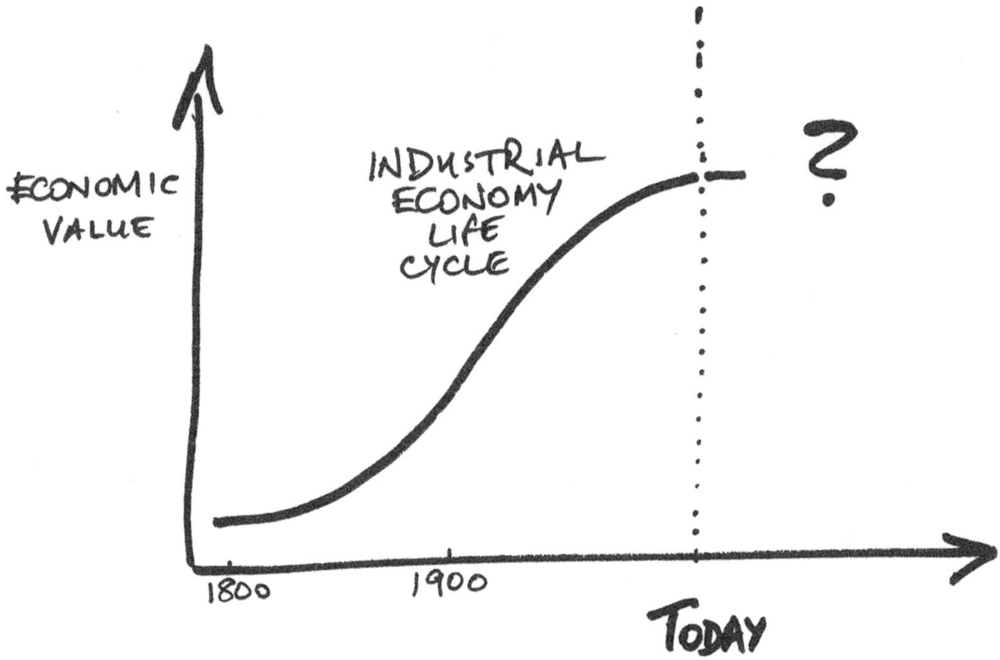

ECONOMIC VALUE
INDUSTRIAL ECONOMY LIFE CYCLE
?
1800
1900
TODAY

Today, we stand at the end of one economic cycle and the start of a threatening tsunami, whose force will shake the foundations of global business and the world economy.

It's not very easy to understand the implications of this powerful economic transformation. Some say we are at the mercy of "the perils of global capitalism!"

The reality is that we now work and live in the context of a "complex dynamic system," a new economy driven by a system of multiple interrelated forces.

It's a crazy world where small economies can have major effects. When the Russian stock market collapsed, shaking economies shook economies worldwide, it was worth less than Wal-Mart! At one stage, Korea's total market cap was less than Dell's!

To understand the new world economy and its impact on your business you must take a systemic, holistic view. Without it, you'll just see disorder, complexity and volatility.

Globalization and deregulation are driving unprecedented openness

Globalization has effectively removed many of the barriers around countries, allowing increasingly free trade and creating more and more consumer choice. Companies can no longer rely on regulation to protect market positions. The leading companies are already competing as if regulations no longer exist.

From a competitive point of view, globalization and deregulation create many new competitors in all markets. The only thing you can be sure of is that your most-feared future competitors will not come from your industry.

Effectively, globalization and deregulation are stripping governments and centrally controlled organizations of power while dramatically increasing the power of the consumer. The individual has unprecedented choice and access to information. Market power is moving inexorably to the individual consumer. This so-called "Sovereign Individual" is demonstrating ever-increasing market power at the expense of governments and large manufacturers. The effect on business, competitiveness, organizations and the very nature of many industries will be profound.

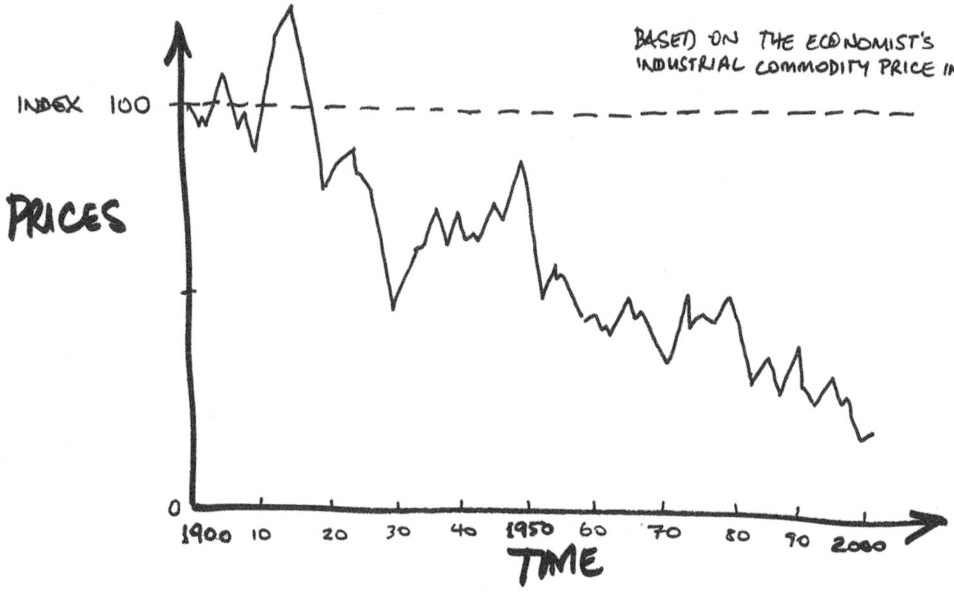
BASED ON THE ECONOMIST'S INDUSTRIAL COMMODITY PRICE INDEX
INDEX 100
PRICES
0
1900 10 20 30 40 1950 60 70 80 90 2000
TIME

Technology has profoundly transformed businesses and markets in the past 40 years.

In the automotive industry, starting during the 1970s, technology applied to the production line increased outputs and decreased costs while improving quality. Eventually, everyone followed the pace set in automation by the Japanese. This industry, like many others driven by technology, is now in a "falling price boom" – it has become increasingly difficult to make a profit.

The falling-price boom

Raw material and commodity prices are lower than at any time in history – *The Economist's* commodity price index shows a drop of 84 percent since 1914 on average. Who would be in these industrial age industries by choice? Half the world's oil companies have disappeared into new merged entities during the last three years. Much of this is directly driven by technology, borderless markets and the smart consumers they create.

Today, almost 300 million people are wired to the Internet. A transistor now costs less than a staple. After 40 years of unbelievable progress, computer technology has finally reached its infancy! The combination of new advances across many areas of technology converging at the cusp of the millennium, will continue to revolutionize business on an unprecedented scale.

The computer and the telecommunications industry have provided the platform for e-commerce. But it is globalization and deregulation that are creating the market context in which e-commerce will flourish.

The Internet is the epitome of "globalness" and "openness"! It has become the implementation platform for global free markets. We have to understand the interdependence of these drivers to understand the inevitability of e-commerce. It is now estimated that e-commerce volumes are doubling every quarter and could exceed $3 trillion–4 trillion per annum by 2005.

In an open, deregulated world market, electronic business will thrive.

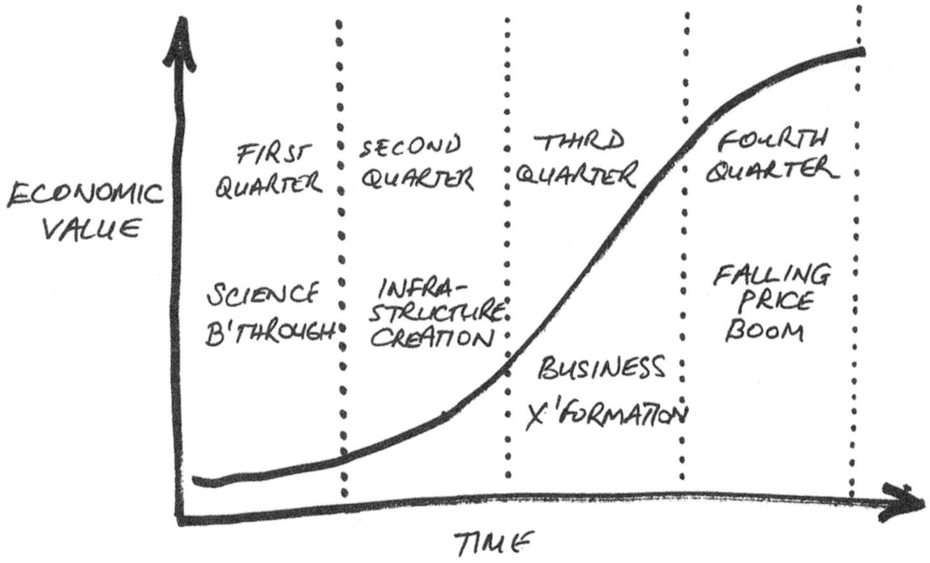
ECONOMIC VALUE
FIRST QUARTER
SECOND QUARTER
THIRD QUARTER
FOURTH QUARTER
SCIENCE B'THROUGH
INFRA-STRUCTURE CREATION
BUSINESS X'FORMATION
FALLING PRICE BOOM
TIME

Economic life cycles

When we step back from the economic phenomena of the past few hundred years, we can see that economies go through life-cycles in much the same way as businesses and people do. An economic life-cycle consists of four quarters, each of which appears to have consistent and predictable characteristics.

In the **First Quarter**, economic value is driven by breakthroughs in science and technology. Think of the internal combustion engine, the transistor, the personal computer. These catalysts may appear over a long period of time, and will have little economic value to begin with. Science and technology, on their own, do not create economies.

It's only in the **Second Quarter** that economic activity begins to take off, with an infrastructure being created around the new science and technology. In the case of the automobile industry, this infrastructure consisted of roads, highways, gas stations, tire manufacturers, driver training, and so on. During this second quarter, economic value is created by companies that build the infrastructure and it is specifically these companies that benefit directly – their shares boom!

Once the infrastructure is in place, in the **Third Quarter** of the economy, changes in economic activity begin affecting *all* companies. Consumers begin reaping the benefits of changing technologies and products. Major businesses are increasingly transformed by the application of the new technologies on their business processes and competitiveness.

In the **Fourth Quarter** of the economy, products and services become ever more commoditized as manufacturing and delivery "secrets" become common knowledge. Previously "leading-edge" technologies become available to anyone, and barriers to entry are lowered. As it is no longer possible to differentiate the commoditizing products and services, companies look for economies of scale and cost-cutting options in a bid to maintain shrinking profit margins. This is the "falling-price boom."

Examples of this are the consolidation of the oil industry and the automobile industry during the last decade of the 20th century. This part of the cycle is also characterized by massive job losses as companies turn increasingly to technology to increase efficiency, cut costs and improve delivery.

After **40** years of

unbelievable progress,

computer technology

has finally

reached its infancy!

The Industrial Economy has been with us for hundreds of years. Our forefathers could be born into this economy, thrive in it and retire in it without experiencing substantial change.

The new Information Economy, often just called the New Economy, driven by communications and computer technologies, has brought more economic transformation in the past decades than the Industrial Economy brought in the past centuries. Clearly the Information Economy was built on the successes of the Industrial Economy, and then leap-frogged the economic impact.

In terms of resources, the Industrial Economy was driven by "the economics of scarcity." Everything that fuelled that economy was in short supply and available only to a few nations. These were the "haves." World wars were fought for access to raw materials, real estate and cheap labor. Later, a more subtle form of economic warfare, colonization, proved effective for European countries in search of these industrial resources.

Industrial Economy Resources	Information Economy Resources
Raw materials	Information
Real estate	Knowledge
Cheap labor	Skills + Ideas

In the Information Economy, the primary resources have become far more intangible and difficult to contain.

Thanks to the Internet, information is no longer a scarce resource. The exploding Information Economy really has created "the economics of plenty"! The challenge now is to keep up with it! Anyone can choose to access all the world's information and turn it into knowledge and skills.

But we must be careful not to overstate the value of information and knowledge in this information-based economy.

The reality is that information has no value, unless it is available immediately before you need it.

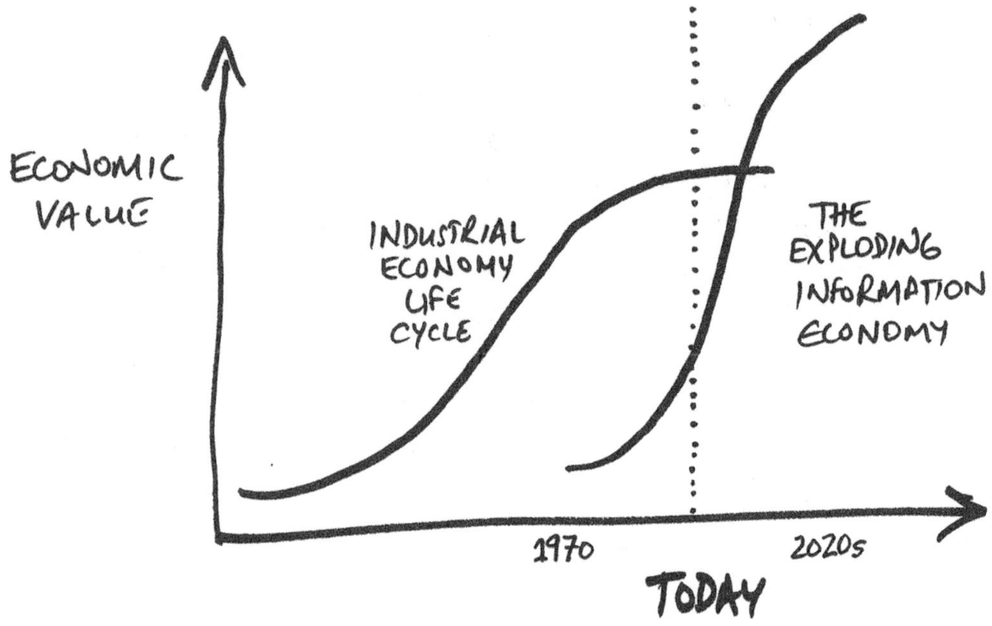
ECONOMIC VALUE
INDUSTRIAL ECONOMY LIFE CYCLE
THE EXPLODING INFORMATION ECONOMY
1970
2020s
TODAY

Information about customers contained in huge databases has absolutely no value, until it is brought to bear immediately before needed at every point of customer contact.

So it is with knowledge.

In this knowledge economy it is clear that knowledge, per se, has no value.

Just look at the salary of the average university professor, and you'll see that this economy does not place a high value on pure knowledge.

However, as soon as that knowledge is turned into a skill, and applied in the real world, this economy places enormous value on it. The new economy is a skills-driven economy, not a knowledge-driven economy. And the only scarcity is *skills*!

There are of course many ex-university professors who have become rich – they "got it"!

Access to information has become a personal choice, rather than a result of belonging to some privileged class. Access to information networks is no longer limited to governments and large corporates, as was the case in the 1970s. Individuals who choose to can now have the same kind of access. Ideas have turned out to be the real fuel of the new economy.

Gone are the days of the "haves" and the "have nots." Today, there are only the "haves" and the "want nots"!

That's why we call it "the economics of attitude." It's your choice, your call. It's not up to someone in central power anymore!

3

Age of the individual

From central control to chaos

“For three days in the sweltering summer of 1969, an event of cataclysmic proportions unfolded on a small patch of farmland in the American state of New York. Half a million people thronged together in the open, as lightning cracked the sky and torrential downpours turned the earth into mud.”

Food and water ran out, traffic choked the freeways, and state troopers and police rushed to the scene as worried authorities declared an emergency. Was it a riot? Was it a revolution? No. It was something much more important. It was Woodstock.

Billed as a festival of "love, peace, and music," starring some of the greatest rock and pop icons of the 1960s, Woodstock transcended its origins to become a lasting symbol of the power of the individual in an age of mass transformation.

Played out against a background of rage, fear, and wonder – man had just set foot on the moon, American soldiers were dying in the jungles of Vietnam, and four young students would soon be gunned down by the National Guard on a campus in Ohio – Woodstock was the epicenter of a Youthquake, the spark that marked the onset of our modern Age of Chaos.

For all the outward evidence of disaster in the making, this blissful yet deafeningly noisy Aquarian festival was a cataclysm in the positive sense of the word: "an event that brings about great and dramatic change."

Entranced by the **vision** of

a fragile blue orb

floating in space,

the children of Woodstock advised us to

defy society's rules

in favor of

doing **our own** thing!

Even today, it is impossible to escape the impact of Woodstock on the restless, rudderless generation who grew up in the shadow of the Bomb.

The flower children of Woodstock, born during the Baby Boom of the late-1940s and 1950s, would grow up to be the visionaries, leaders, and entrepreneurs who chart the course of our planet today.

Bill Clinton, twice-President of the USA, is a child of Woodstock. So is the UK's Tony Blair. So is South African President Thabo Mbeki. So are Steven Spielberg, Mick Jagger and Gloria Steinheim.

It may not have looked like it at the time, but Woodstock was far more than a platform for free love, skinnydipping, amphetamines, and rock 'n' roll. It was a catalyst for the surge of antiwar sentiment that would drive the world's greatest military power from the heat of a hopeless conflict in Southeast Asia.

It was a tribal gathering of young people who were profoundly aware of their rights in a free society, and fiercely convinced that they held in their hands the power to change the world. The fate of nations, they decided, was too important to be entrusted to politicians. People Power – the power of ordinary individuals, with extraordinary dreams and ideals – was the best recipe for radical change and action.

Entranced by the vision of a fragile blue orb floating in space, as captured on film and bounced back home by the Apollo astronauts, the children of Woodstock advised us to "Make Love, Not War," to "Tune In, Turn On, and Drop Out," and, perhaps most importantly, to defy society's deeply-entrenched rules and conventions in favor of doing our own thing.

Many took the advice to heart. Among them, a young man named William Henry Gates, who dropped out of Harvard in his junior year to pursue his teenage obsession with electronics and computer programming.

In 1975, gripped by the far-fetched notion of "a computer on every desktop," he started a modest little company called Microsoft. The rest is not history... the rest is the *future*.

No longer

can we

afford to seek

sanctuary in what we know,

or what has gone before.

Likewise, it was two scruffy-haired high school dropouts, Steven Jobs and Steven Wozniak, who joined forces in 1976 to build a desktop computer with a name that evoked an instant return to the Garden of Eden.

Today, Microsoft and Apple Computer Inc, reincarnated as a business success in a kind of "second coming" by Steve Jobs, stand at the helm of an unstoppable revolution in the way we use, perceive, and disseminate information, and in turn, the way the global economy is driving and changing our world.

It is not too difficult, with the benefit of 20-20 hindsight, to draw a direct line between those three days of mud and music on Max Yasgur's farm, and the dramatic rise of the Internet as the ultimate forum for doing your own thing. Starting a global business, publishing your own magazine, kicking off a worldwide campaign against industrial pollution… you name it, you can do it.

In the aftershock of Woodstock's spirit of communal idealism and individual power, we can also trace the reverberations that would lead to the destruction of the Berlin Wall and the fall of Apartheid in South Africa; to civil rights and consumer power.

But let's be honest: for all its influence, real and symbolic, direct and indirect, on the society that gave it birth, Woodstock in the flesh must have been three days of undiluted, non-stop chaos. That's just the point. It was chaos! And that's exactly why it worked.

Chaos is not just an **overturned truck** on a freeway, or a **horde of shoppers** fighting over bargains at a summer sale, or a **rock musician** smashing his guitar against a smoldering amplifier. **Chaos is life.**

Chaos is a focal point for the natural, omnipresent forces that shape and define our world. You'll find the evidence in headlines and TV reports of fires, floods, hurricanes, and other everyday catastrophes. But you'll also find them in the random, defiantly unpredictable nature of markets and economies. Take a look for yourself…

- *The Russian stock market collapses, losing 90 percent of its value in less than a year.*

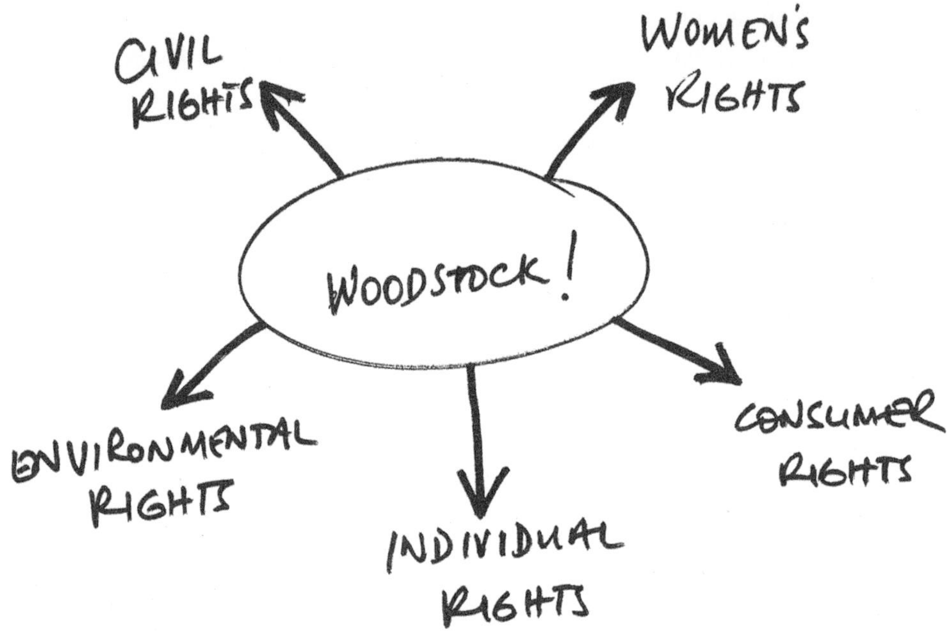
CIVIL RIGHTS
WOMEN'S RIGHTS
WOODSTOCK!
ENVIRONMENTAL RIGHTS
INDIVIDUAL RIGHTS
CONSUMER RIGHTS

- *The currency of Indonesia, once one of the world's most stable economies, plunges by 73 percent in just six months.*
- *On Wall Street, the Dow Jones is shaken by its biggest single-day loss ever.*
- *In Asia, the semiconductor market takes a drastic knock, with prices tumbling 25 percent in two months.*
- *Japan, traditionally the most robust of Asian Tigers, battles against the threat of deflation and depression. Japan's value drops from 50 percent to 14 percent of world markets in less than a decade.*
- *Around the world, markets are characterized by huge oversupply – everything from automobiles to oil, semiconductors to bandwidth, is being made available in large quantities at ever-shrinking costs.*

In the language of Chaos Theory, Woodstock was a bifurcation point – a point at which all the rules suddenly changed!

Think of it in terms of the flow of water from your kitchen faucet – first it flows smoothly and predictably and then, as you open the faucet fully, there is sudden turbulence. Immediately, you're faced with a new set of rules that fluid mechanics cannot explain, a new complexity that can only be understood within the context of Chaos!

As the hit sixties comedy put it, it's a mad, mad, mad, mad world. Everything is haphazard. Erratic. Capricious. No longer can we afford to seek sanctuary in what we know, or what has gone before. We need to learn from what's going to happen; we need to absorb and apply the lessons of the future.

As much as I'd like to, I'm afraid I can't tell you exactly what lies in store in that not-so-distant territory. But this much I can say for sure: it's going to be chaotic. And you won't be able to escape the madness, wherever in the world you may be. The new global economy is a tightly woven web of interconnected, interdependent nodes and hot-zones, governed by what scientists like to call the "Butterfly Effect."

The most self-assured forecast of a **bull-run** in Johannesburg can **be thrown** to the winds by a broker **sneezing** at his keyboard in Singapore.

The Butterfly Effect

A tiny butterfly flaps its wings in a park in Beijing, setting in motion a chain of minute disturbances, shifts, and variations that lead directly to a massive thunderstorm in New York a month later. The Butterfly Effect, a term coined by a physicist to explain the effects of unimaginably "complex dynamic systems," is commonly used to explain why it is so difficult to predict the weather more than a few days in advance.

Apply the same principle to economics, and you can see why the most self-assured forecast of a bull-run on Wall Street can be thrown to the winds by a broker sneezing at his keyboard in Singapore. Result? Chaos.

All around the world, barriers are being lifted, borders are being opened, industries are being deregulated. Market power is moving from the giant conglomerates to the individual consumer, as information and communications technologies enable almost anyone, anywhere, to tap into a vibrant and hungry global marketplace.

From expert advice to herd behavior

Time and distance hardly enter the equation anymore. Nor does personal wealth. At the turn of the 20th century, most capital flows could be traced back to a few thousand wealthy families. Today they are driven by hundreds of millions of individual investors, some of whom were collectively responsible for creating the phenomenal growth in the emerging Tiger Economies of the Far East. This is "herd behavior" in action. Often values are determined by the chaotic swarm behavior of millions of individual investors rather than by deliberate rational thought of the expert advisers of the Industrial Age.

But these small investors are a fickle force, quick to disinvest and channel their money into hot new markets. Africa? South America? China? Only the butterfly knows for sure. The rest of us, craving some semblance of order, harmony, and structure in our lives, will instinctively fight and resist the chaos all around. That would be wrong.

Far better to embrace the chaos; to learn from it; to make it work for us, rather than against us. Look back at Woodstock. Just as there is a strange, jarring beauty to be found in the upside-down, inside-out version of The Star-Spangled Banner played by Jimi Hendrix, so there is meaning to be found in the madness of the markets, and so there are mesmerizing patterns to be discerned in the volatile disorder of the natural world.

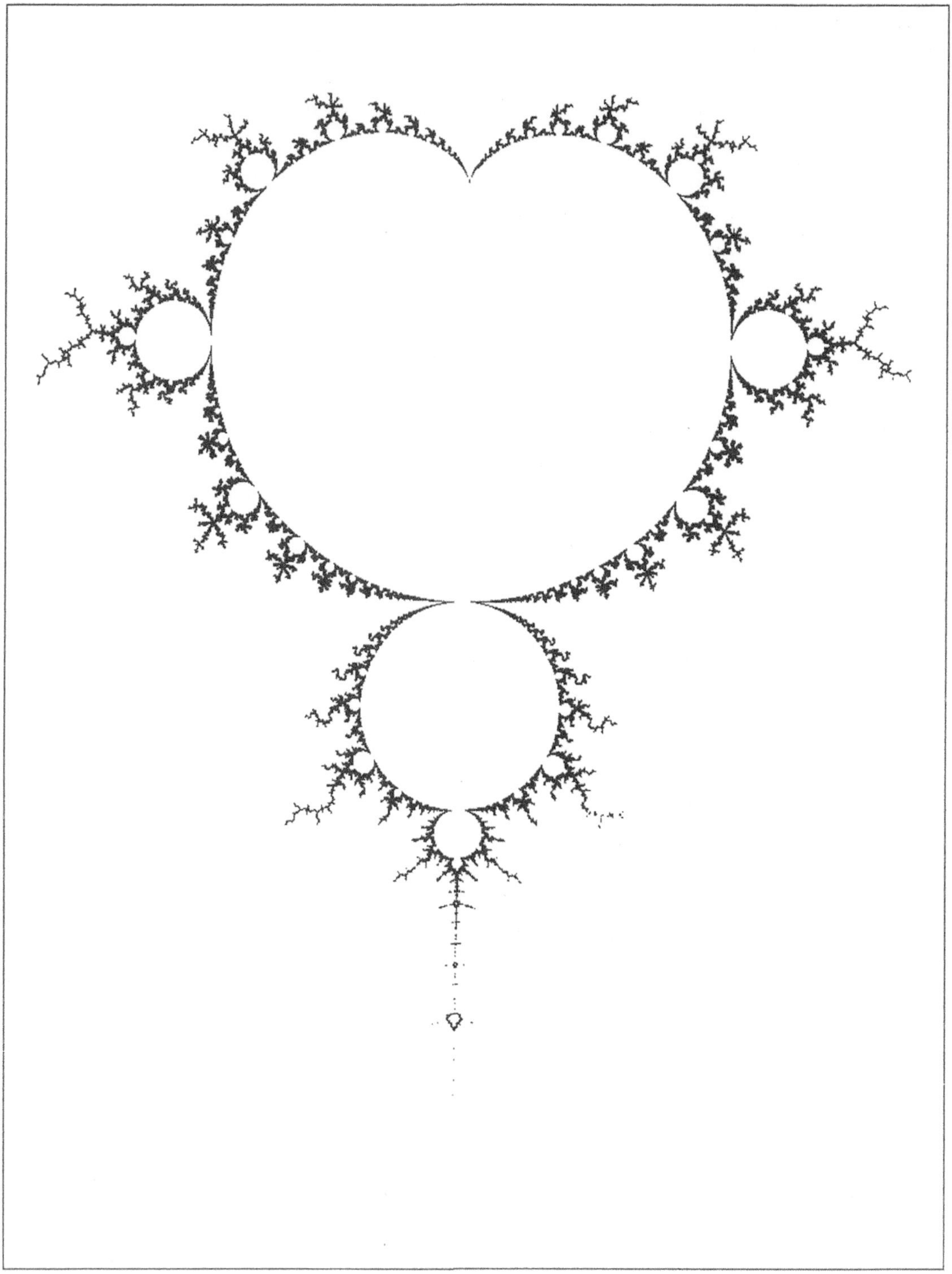

A fractal world

Consider the fractal. A particle of colored light generated on a computer screen by some of the most complex mathematical equations known to mankind, creating shifting, kaleidoscopic patterns in a universe of chaos.

When Benoit Mandelbrot discovered the fractal nature of the world and presented his famed "Mandelbrot Set" as the start of the new geometry of life, it was really just about pleasingly symmetrical shapes etched on computer screens.

Now we see that the fractal forms a perfect analogy of business success and organisational structure in the new global economy.

Gone are the rigid, pyramid hierarchies of yesteryear; in their place, a range of flexible, adaptable, lean and mean organizations, whittled down to their smallest individual components in this age of increasing decentralization and deregulation.

Our central control models, born of the Industrial Economy, simply can't do the job for us anymore. They're lumbering, antiquated, mechanistic. Increasingly, the markets of the Information Economy are exhibiting the characteristics of the complex, dynamic systems that shape the world around us. A world born in chaos.

The very word chaos takes us back to the formless void that preceded the Big Bang – and the Big Bang isn't over yet! Every day, we find ourselves having to deal with the random, unpredictable forces of change. Every day, we have to weigh up the dilemma between structure on the one hand, and chaos on the other. It's a dilemma as old as civilization itself.

The worlds of Horus and Seth

The Egyptian Museum in Cairo houses a mind-numbing number of artefacts that shed light on the way people lived and worshipped in the Nile Delta some three to seven millennia ago. In one particularly dimly lit corner of the museum, I found a little-known statue of a pharaoh being counseled by two deities.

On the left is *Horus*, the god of structure and predictability. On the right: *Seth*, the god of chaos and disorder. Even thousands of years ago, the conflict between order and chaos, and the dilemmas created for those in authority, were well recognized.

In a very real sense, today's business executive is in the same position as that stone pharaoh. Everything we have been taught about business was crafted in the Industrial Age – in an economy where central authority, predictability and control were the touchstones.

We are the sons and daughters of Horus.
But we are living in Seth's world!

Take a look at this table...

Industrial Age "Culture" in the Age of Horus	Information Age "Spirit" in the Age of Seth
Learn a skill	Lifelong learning
Security	Risk-taking
Job preservation	Job creation
Capital equipment	Intellectual capital
Status quo	Speed and change
Hierarchical and regulated	Distributed and networked
Zero sum	Win–win
Measure inputs	Measure outputs

The unwieldy corporate *cultures* of the Industrial Economy are rapidly being replaced by a kind of *team spirit* especially suitable to the new e-commerce organizations of today – swift, nimble and driven by almost religious visions of the future – "Don't look for profits here, we want to change the world!"

From a temple on the Nile to a muddy field in Woodstock, from a footprint on the moon to a domain name on the world wide web, we remain a restless, rudderless species, questing for meaning, questing for answers, questing to find the best way forward.

Let's set forward in the spirit of Woodstock and Seth.

The future begins now!

4

Disruptive technology

Catalysts for economic revolution

"Do you remember where you were and what you were doing on July 20, 1969? I do. Like millions of other people on Planet Earth, I was transfixed by the sight of another member of my species setting foot on the dry, powdery surface of our nearest celestial neighbor."

As I watched the ghostly flicker of the live television images, and I heard the distant crackle of Neil Armstrong's voice – "That's one small step for a man, one giant leap for mankind" – I was awed by the grandeur of human achievement and the unstoppable power of science and technology.

Even now, across the gulf of time and space, the moon landing stands out as the most compelling example of our collective ability to breach the boundaries of the possible.

But perhaps the most remarkable aspect of Armstrong's first footfall, seen in the light of the many giant leaps we have taken since then, is that it was made possible entirely without the use of microprocessors. In our Digital Age, that's hard to imagine.

Even the Concorde, the sleek supersonic jetliner that has now become just another form of commuter transport, first took flight in 1971 without the benefit of these now-ubiquitous electronic marvels. We've come a long way.

The great irony is that every giant leap has made our world a smaller place, with consumer technology itself shrinking in size and price at a rate that is just about impossible to monitor.

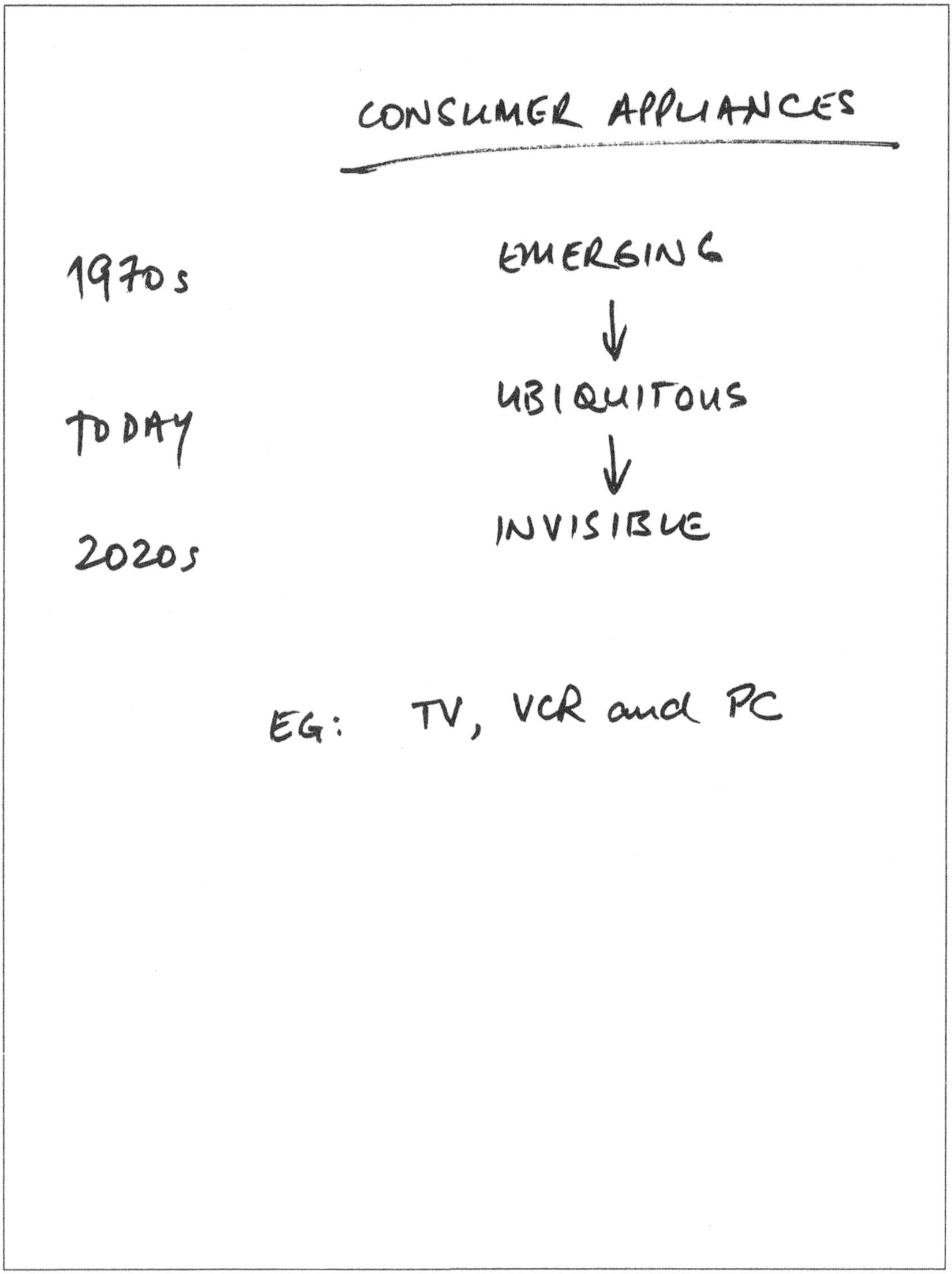
CONSUMER APPLIANCES
1970s
EMERGING
TODAY
UBIQUITOUS
2020s
INVISIBLE
EG: TV, VCR and PC

Huge mainframe computers, once the size of a room, have given way to desktops, laptops, palmtops, and PDAs. Circular slabs of double-sided black vinyl, 12 inches in diameter, have given way to pristine-sounding CDs and MiniDiscs.

Giant radio receivers with glowing, humming valves have given way to transistor radios that are tiny enough to plug into your ear. Home video camcorders, once cumbersome enough to give you backache, can now fit easily into the palm of your hand. And if you don't own a pocket-sized cellphone, for personal or business use, you must be living on another planet.

But all this is only the beginning. Today, you don't even need a radio to listen to the radio. You can tune into your personal choice of news, talk, and music from around the world, simply by clicking in the right place on your Internet browser. Nor do you need a CD player to catch up on the latest pop hits.

Digital music, in the form of highly compressed MP3 files, can be downloaded at leisure for playback through your computer speakers, or through tiny solid-state devices such as Diamond's Rio MP3 player.

The easy accessibility of commercial music, software, and other copyrighted material on the Internet has sent waves of panic through industries that were once able to exercise strict control over the flow and distribution of information.

But there's no holding back the tide. By 2020, such commonplace devices as the radio, CD player, and VCR will seem quaint and antiquated, as we enjoy instant access to music, movies, and television in our homes, offices, and even our cars, simply by downloading the necessary data as and when we require it.

Content will become intangible and pervasive. The quality of transmission will be crystal-clear and digitally perfect. By the time we make our next giant leap into the Great Unknown – with a manned landing on the surface of Mars, perhaps – the ghostly flicker of Apollo 11 will be nothing but the shadow of a distant memory. Thanks to the power of science and technology, the future will look and sound brighter than we can possibly imagine.

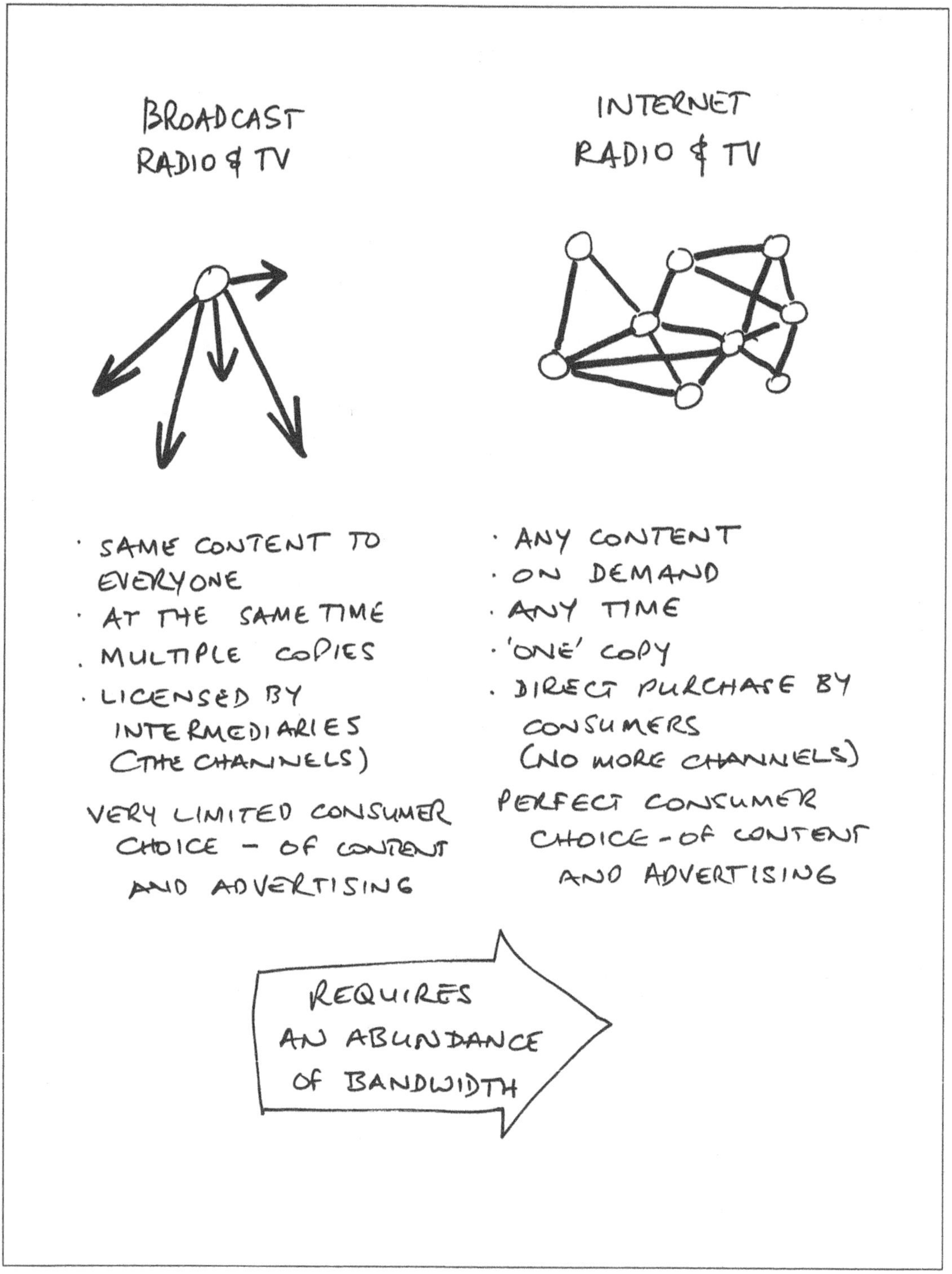
BROADCAST RADIO & TV
INTERNET RADIO & TV
· SAME CONTENT TO EVERYONE
· AT THE SAME TIME
· MULTIPLE COPIES
· LICENSED BY INTERMEDIARIES (THE CHANNELS)
VERY LIMITED CONSUMER CHOICE – OF CONTENT AND ADVERTISING
· ANY CONTENT
· ON DEMAND
· ANY TIME
· 'ONE' COPY
· DIRECT PURCHASE BY CONSUMERS (NO MORE CHANNELS)
PERFECT CONSUMER CHOICE – OF CONTENT AND ADVERTISING
REQUIRES AN ABUNDANCE OF BANDWIDTH

Let's take a closer look at some of the changes and developments that lie in store.

Say goodbye to your VCR and TV channels

Next to your television set – or, more likely, just underneath it – the video cassette recorder is the most commonplace electronic appliance in the average switched-on household. It's great for watching rented movies, taping live broadcasts, or fast-forwarding through ads and other unwanted material. But in the late 1960s, the home VCR was just a distant dream.

Video recorders were the size of a small room, until Sony scaled them down to the size of a large table-top. The first Sony Betamax, designed for home use, was launched in the USA in 1975. The home video explosion had begun.

The first digital VCRs hit the market in 1999, although they still use fragile, degradable magnetic tape as a storage medium. The advent of DVD (Digital Versatile Disk) as a movie playback medium signaled the slow but sure demise of the VCR. Recordable DVDs are already widely used in the professional arena.

By 2020, VCRs will not be in use anymore. In fact the VCR "product" will have turned into a "service" available in your satellite or cable decoder. Click the remote to record and the movie will be stored on a chip in the decoder. Click to playback at any time and a small amount will be charged to your monthly satellite service.

Eventually though, the whole concept of broadcast channels will disappear. As radio and television programming is increasingly delivered "on demand" directly to listeners and viewers through the Internet infrastructure, the pressure on the broadcast channels will increase. High costs with fewer and fewer viewers to support them. Once bandwidth becomes plentiful and cheap (essentially "free" within about five years) there will be no reason to subscribe to *any* channel, because all content will be available "on demand," directly from the originator of the content! From producer to viewer without any intermediaries.

As television becomes a sub-set of the Internet,
all channels will disappear.
No more CNN, BBC or CBS.

Only the content origination business will survive – there will always be a vast market for direct sales of news, movies and series. But the broadcast infrastructure, and all suppliers who depend on it, will cease to exist.

Let's take a look at the changing face of home entertainment globally since the days of the moon landing.

1970s	Today	2020s
One TV for every 25 people in the world	One TV for every four people in the world	TV=PC, displays everywhere
Hundreds of TV channels	Thousands of TV channels	No TV channels
The VCR is an industrial item, available only to professionals	TV and the VCR are the most common appliances	The VCR is a relic of the distant past
	Explosion of digital, portable consumer appliances	Consumer appliances become services
	Direct distribution of content via the Internet	TV is a subset of the Internet

A computer (or two) on every desktop

In 1970, the computer was anything but "personal." It was big, bulky, and as slow by today's standards as a stegosaurus. The somewhat apprehensive start of the personal computer revolution can be traced to the launch of the Altair 8800 in January 1975.

Apple was founded the following year by Steve Jobs and Steve Wozniak, two Californian college drop-outs. They launched the Apple II personal computer in 1977. It had no keyboard, no display, no operating system, and no application software. You had to be really determined to want to use it!

But the Apple was just a taste of things to come, the appetizer for a revolution that would be heralded by the launch of the IBM PC in 1981. Cloned at

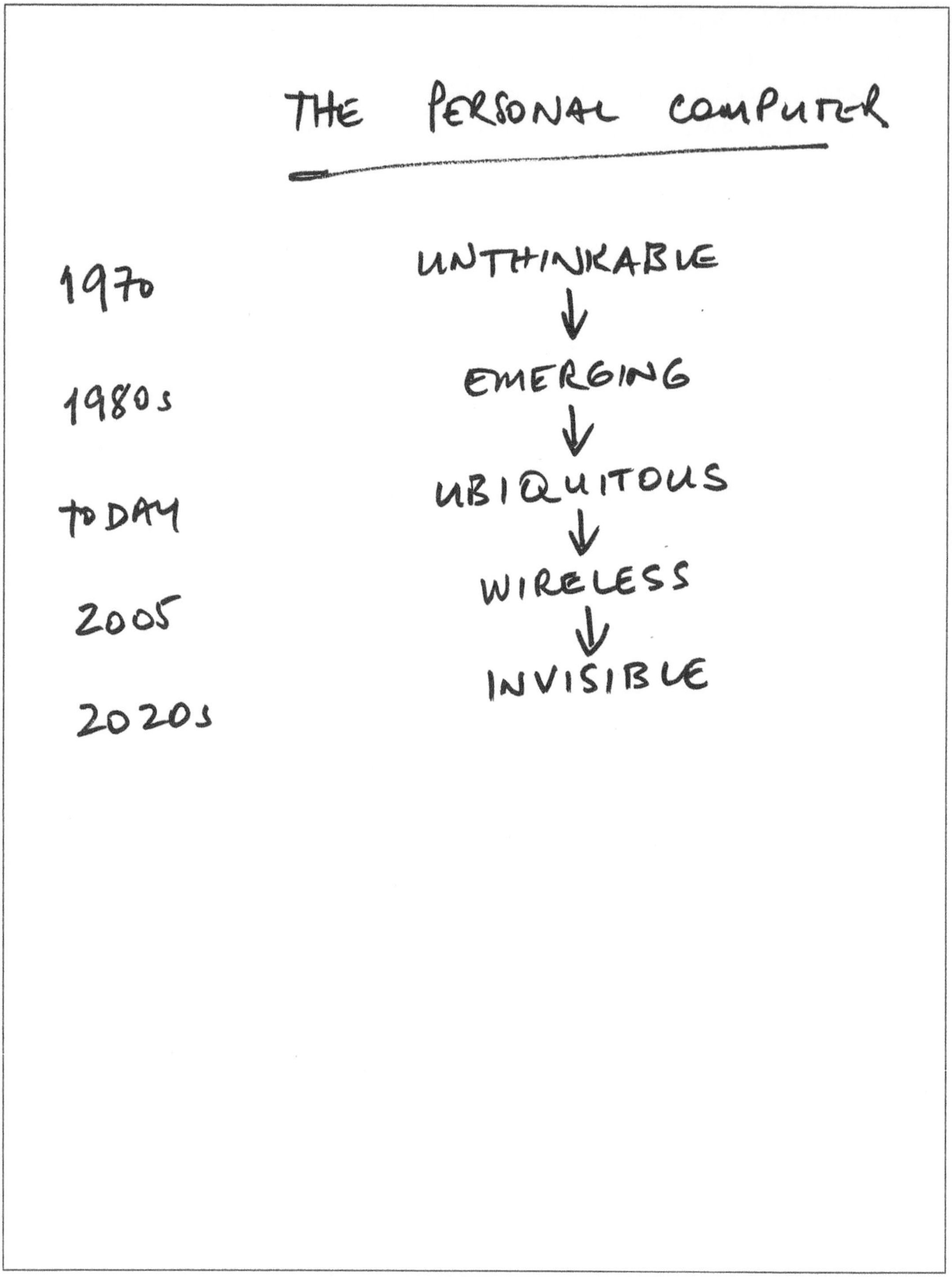
THE PERSONAL COMPUTER
1970
UNTHINKABLE
1980s
EMERGING
TODAY
UBIQUITOUS
2005
WIRELESS
2020s
INVISIBLE

low cost by Asian manufacturers, the PC brought undreamed-of processing power to the home and home office, forever changing the way people work, network, and access information.

The vision of "a computer on every desktop," as voiced by Microsoft founder Bill Gates, has proved to be inaccurate only in its lack of ambition. It's not uncommon for home users to have a computer on the desktop, a laptop for the road, and a palmtop in the pocket, allowing them to exchange information and stay in touch no matter where in the world they may be.

The next step in the evolution of the PC will be its integration with the digital cellphone, setting the stage for the second round of a technological conflict that has gripped the hearts and minds of millions.

Everything — the PC, telephones, consumer appliances, home entertainment, vending machines and *you* – will eventually be connected into the worlds evolving digital skin. Billions of interconnected devices that will create a ubiquitous nervous system for the planet.

For most people in the world their first contact with the Internet will come via a cellphone.

Today the world is growing a **digital skin** – a **nervous system** on the back of which **smart** electronic businesses **will flourish!**

1970s	Today	2020s
Telephones – Wired: 200m – Wireless: < 1m All analog	Telephones – Wired: 750m – Wireless: 400m Mostly analog (especially in USA and Japan)	Telephones – Wired: 1,000m – Wireless: 2,000m All digital
One phone for every 18 people	One phone for every 5 people	One phone for every 3 people
Telephone number is a place	Telephone number is a person (personal phone)	No more telephone numbers or e-mail addresses. Your name.com becomes the most valuable resource.
	Bandwidth is scarce	Bandwidth is free
Birth of consumer electronics	Proliferation of consumer devices	The end of consumer devices
Telephone infrastructure dominant	Telephone, TV and Internet infrastructures dominant	"Everyone" is connected
Telephone infrastructure exploding	Digital wireless infrastructure exploding	Wireless access dominant
	E-commerce is a key competitive differentiator	E-commerce is no longer a competitive differentiator. You're either an e-business, or have gone out of business.

From being the

most wired region

on the planet in 1900,

Scandinavia has today

become the

most wireless!

Telecommunications and the Internet wars

In the last half of the 1990s, American computer companies dominated the development of hardware, software, infrastructure and emerging e-commerce markets. Nasdaq became the icon for youthful and rampant economic success. Forty percent of American homes had PCs, and more than half of those were connected to the Internet. The two-PC family seemed as natural as the two-car family of the 1970s. Europe and Asia ran a very poor second.

Then, during 1999, in a development that was largely ignored by American commentators, the battleground for control of the Internet began switching to Europe.

The explosive growth of digital cellphone markets, driven by GSM technology, took many by surprise. The most optimistic forecasts were surpassed.

Scandinavia became the epicenter of the digital cellphone revolution, and Finland's Nokia briefly surpassed BP-Amoco as Europe's most valuable business. A few months later the merged Vodafone and Mannesman surpassed Nokia, putting cellphone companies in #1 and #2 positions in the European market capitalization stakes.

But none of this should really have come as a surprise. Even in 1900, Scandinavia had the highest concentration of telephones per capita in the world. Stockholm had more telephones than London or Berlin. From being the most wired region on the planet, Scandinavia has today also become the most wireless.

Today, the American and Japanese cellphone markets are still the biggest in the world. The irony is that their early start has left them lagging in the technology race. They're stuck with outmoded analog systems that do not provide the same security and opportunity for development as digital.

The GSM digital cellphone even has advantages over a PC. The SIM card provides positive personal identification through passwords, making it an

The cellphone will become the preferred payment infrastructure within a decade ideal and pervasive device for electronic payments of all kinds, from electricity bills to parking meters and soft drinks to grocery purchases.

Also, the cellphone is effectively an increasingly more precise global positioning system – the networks know precisely where in which "cell" you are! Combine the ability to pay with the sense of location and you have a scenario for a powerful new interface to the network.

The year is 2002, you are strolling around a large shopping mall and your cellphone tells you that it has detected that two of your friends (based on a scan of your list of frequently dialled numbers) have just entered the same shopping mall. In fact, the same message has gone out to all three: "Would you like to meet for a coffee?" A simple "Yes" response (hit the green button!) gives each the same instruction: "Let's meet at the coffee shop on Level 2?" Clearly this is a bit of value added advertising sponsored by the coffee shop. Is this kind of "intrusion" desirable? Your kids will love it! Just think of the plethora of new applications.

But the scenario is not yet complete. The coffee shop has no till, just a note to say "Dial 123 to pay your bill." No credit card required. Just key in the amount and your PIN and the transaction is complete. No fuss. No credit card!

The big difference in this scenario is what happens in the back office. The transactions are now processed by your cellphone service provider, rather than your bank, and will appear on your cellphone account at the end of the month. Instead of the bank processing hundreds of thousands of credit card transactions daily, they may only process of few hundred settlement instructions as the cellphone service providers become the new payment intermediaries.

In fact, digital cellphones pose a very real and immediate threat to the credit card industry and the growth of the smart card market around the world.

Why on earth have a credit card or a smart card, if the card inside your cellphone can perform the same functions, off-line and online, at a far lower cost, on an existing infrastructure? The cellphone may well become the preferred payment infrastructure within a decade and the cellphone service providers may become the new consumer banks! Master Card and Visa beware!

The Europeans, with their experience in digital cellphones and their dominant penetration in the use of these devices, clearly have the opportunity to win the second round of the Internet War!

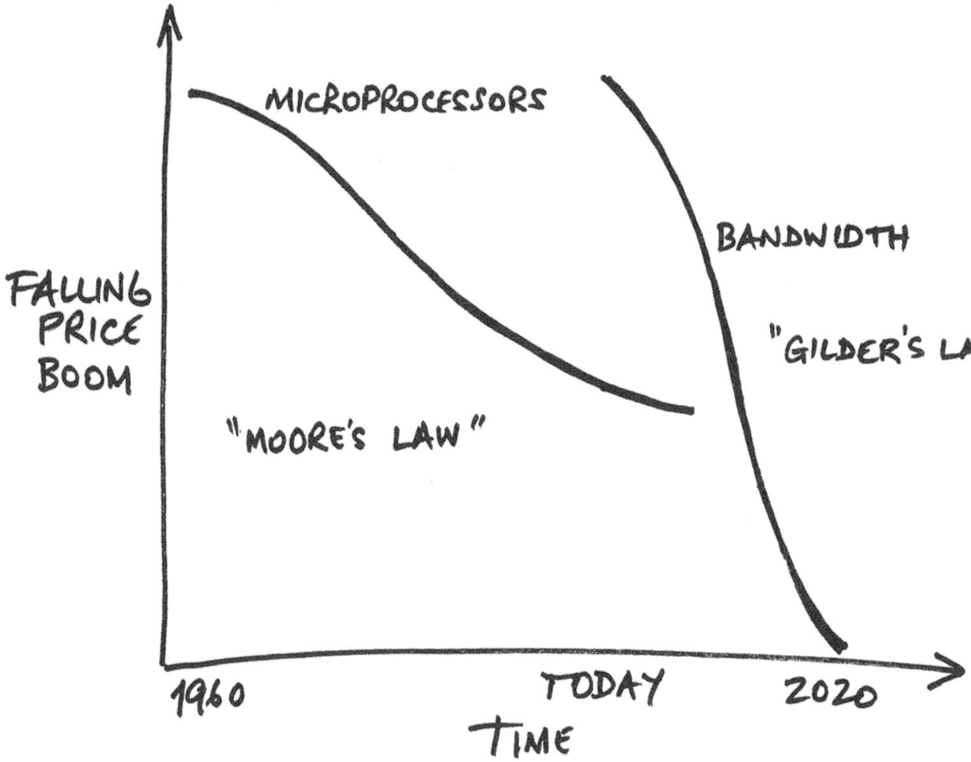
MICROPROCESSORS
BANDWIDTH
FALLING PRICE BOOM
"GILDER'S LAW"
"MOORE'S LAW"
1960
TODAY
2020
TIME

The UK-based electronics company, Psion, a maker of hand-held personal information appliances, effected a coup by getting the world's largest cellphone manufacturers to become partners in Symbian, a new joint venture to develop operating systems for digital cellphone devices.

Bandwidth has always been considered a major limitation with wireless technology, but by 2002, a speed of two megabits per second will be commonplace. That's 40 times faster than the current top speed of your 56kps PC modem. Suddenly, you'll be able to watch live television on your cellphone!

By then, sales of digital web-enabled cellphones and their derivatives, running the Symbian operating systems, will outstrip sales of personal computers by an order of magnitude.

This wireless Internet may well be **dominated** by European companies, in every area from **hardware to software**, from **massive infrastructure** providers to new service companies. **The opportunity** is there for the taking!

In a sense, the digital revolution in telecommunications has already started. Moore's Law – microprocessor power doubles every 18 months – drove the falling-price boom in the computer industry. In the same way Gilder's Law – available bandwidth will *treble* every 12 months – will send the bandwidth industry into an unprecedented price spiral, as a plethora of new services enter the market on the back of an almost free infrastructure.

The value of any electronic device increases exponentially as it connects to the world's digital skin. Take the humble door bell, for example. If someone rings it and no-one's at home, it turns out to be a useless device. However, if your doorbell was connected to the digital skin, it could cause your cellphone to ring. You could talk to the "ringer" and decide whether to unlock the door and let them in remotely. After all, it could be your son who has locked himself out.

And so the march of technology continues, with innovation and imagination striding boldly forward, in step.

Beyond lies a world where

miniature

computers will be

manufactured atom by atom,

molecule by molecule, to be

embedded

wherever, whenever, and in whoever.

Miniaturization will continue to astonish us. Even today, a tiny computer has been developed, capable of serving as a fully-functional web-server, with a microprocessor that is no bigger than a match-head. Beyond this lies a world where miniature computers will be manufactured atom by atom, molecule by molecule, to be embedded wherever, whenever, and in whoever.

From our perspective in 2020, today's typical PC will be seen as little more than a transient step in the evolution of the first truly "personal" computer – a device that will literally get under your skin, and stay there as an inextricable part of every moment of your life. You will have your own personal web-server implanted just below your epidermis. It will remind you when you have mail and will transmit messages and or movie clips directly via your nervous system to your visual cortex for instant viewing – perfectly, no matter what the quality of your eyes.

Think about a future where you won't even have to think about computers, because they'll be too small to be seen by the naked eye. Welcome to the brave new universe... of nanotechnology.

It's a small, small, small, small world

How small is small? Just how tiny is tiny? When we shift our focus from the infinite to the infinitesimal, we usually narrow our world down to "microscopic" proportions. But you can't use a microscope to see the really tiny stuff. Atoms, for example, the building-blocks of our universe, are smaller than the wavelength of light. That's when our world shrinks to "nanoscopic" dimensions.

The root of the word, "nano," stands for "billionth," which is a million times smaller than the quantity represented by the much more familiar "micro." We're talking really, really small here. But at the same time, we're talking about the Next Big Thing in the technological revolution of the early 21st century.

Nanotechnology.

Imagine a world without poverty. Without disease. Without hunger. A world where armies of silent, invisible robots, programmed to manipulate and rearrange atoms one by one, could assemble anything from a truck to a beefsteak to a computer, or travel through your bloodstream to tinker with your cells and reverse the processes that cause illness and ageing.

It sounds like science-fiction, and for now, it is. But the basis of the fantasy is a simple, everyday fact: everything in the universe is made up of billions upon billions of atomic molecules. Change the order of the molecules, insert a different one here and there, juggle them around a bit, and you can conquer the scourge of HIV or turn a tuft of grass into a prime cut of fillet.

Far-fetched? Not when you consider that the very same process is used to turn chunks of black coal into glittering diamonds, or grains of desert sand into the silicon chips at the heart of every electronic device.

The nascent science of nanotechnology, which envisions endless production lines of nano-robots, shift-shaping items atom by atom, brings within our grasp the alchemy of a whole new age.

One of the leading scientists working in the field, Eric Drexler, told a US Senate subcommittee that the first practical applications of nanotechnology could be on the market as early as 2007. It's hard to say what form the applications will take, although the likeliest areas of development are medicine and computing. Either way, the building blocks of the revolution are already firmly in place.

And yet, it wasn't until the mid-1980s that humankind was able to get its first real glimpse inside the molecular structure of the universe as we know it.

The age

of the Designer Molecule

has arrived.

The invention of the Scanning Tunnelling Microscope (STM) brought man eye-to-eye with the atom, and earned a Nobel Prize for its inventors, Binnin and Rohrer of IBM.

The two scientists were able to create the first visual images of atoms by scanning their microscope across a surface and using the probe to "tunnel" between the atoms. But the real breakthrough came with the discovery that the STM was capable of a whole lot more than merely making the invisible visible. It could also be used to stir individual atoms into action, a thesis Binnin and Rohrer put to the test by herding a host of molecules into the shape of the IBM logo.

Behind this seemingly frivolous exercise in corporate loyalty and brand-building, lay a range of possibilities that could quite literally change the shape of the world as we know it. The age of the Designer Molecule had arrived. If an STM could be used to store and read digital data, for instance, you'd be able to fit more than a trillion bits of information on an area as big as a postage stamp. That's every volume of the Encyclopedia Brittanica – multiplied 500 times!

Likewise, nanotechnology will allow you to build a transistor from a single molecule of carbon, or store the equivalent of one million one-gigabyte hard drives on a single fingernail-sized disk. Just as we no longer blink twice at the sight of a CD-ROM containing the collected works of Shakespeare, so will these now-staggering developments become part of the everyday landscape of our Information Society.

Nanotechnology has the potential to alter our world in ways we cannot even imagine. The ability to toy with molecules, as if they were Lego-blocks, will lead us from the Atomic Age into the Sub-Atomic Age. The implications will be earth-shattering – only this time, we will be manipulating atoms to create, rather than destroy.

For now, our understanding of technology is that it is used to make things. But as soon as we begin thinking on a nano scale, and as soon as we transform that thinking into practice, we will find ourselves moving from the world of the "made" into the world of the "born."

This raises an interesting series of moral and practical dilemmas. Are we really ready to be the masters of our own domain?

The BioTech revolution

In the aftermath of World War Two, a bright new age of prosperity dawned on the face of America. For the nuclear family – mother, father, daughter, son, maybe a couple of pets – happiness was a home in the suburbs, with a neatly

trimmed garden, a refrigerator in the kitchen, and a wood-paneled station-wagon in the driveway. But in the distance, invisible to the naked eye, a cloud was hovering over the horizon. A cloud... shaped like a mushroom.

The Cold War between the USA and Russia, combined with the headlong rush into uncharted space, ushered in an era of paranoia that provided endless fuel for science-fiction writers and prophets of doom. What if the Russians launched a nuclear attack? What if bug-eyed aliens invaded the earth? What if giant robots took over our homes?

Today we can afford to laugh at these fears, even as we blush at the memory of otherwise sober-minded citizens taking to the hills to escape the devastating effects of the Millennium Bug. As a species, we tend to fear change and the advent of new technologies, as much as we ultimately come to embrace them.

At the start of this eagerly awaited 21st century, we're no longer worried about robots and bombs. Instead, our fears revolve around the awesome power we hold to create people in our own image, as we tamper with plants and animals to unleash a new breed of genetically mutated monsters...

Frankenstein foods!

If you read the tabloids, watch the talk shows, and follow the Internet newsgroups, you'll see that few contemporary issues have as much power to stir emotion as genetic engineering and the modification of foodstuffs.

Activists argue that the benefits of Genetic Modification have not been sufficiently proven, and that the practice could have harmful side-effects on the environment. "Plant Liberation" groups have systematically destroyed fields of genetically modified crops in England, while supermarket chains in a number of countries have removed GM products from their shelves in response to consumer protests.

On the other side of the divide, advocates of Genetic Modification argue that more robust, more resilient strains of plant life could go a long way

DNA exists in every cell of every living being. It is the architect of life itself, the blueprint for everything we are. It is the software of all living things.

towards alleviating food shortages in a world struck by poverty and famine. But whatever the merits of the debate, the truth is that mankind has been manipulating living organisms for thousands of years.

The ancient Egyptians put yeast into bread, brewed beer, and used plants to extract minerals from the soil. For more than 500 years, farmers have been selectively breeding the best possible crops in a wide variety of climatic conditions. Since 1920 alone, crop yields have increased sixfold on a global basis.

Today we stand on the threshold of a new agrarian revolution, thanks to the discovery of the myriad of possibilities that lie intertwined in the double-helix of Deoxyribose Nucleic Acid. It was only in 1953 that the now-familiar 3D structure of DNA was discovered by two Nobel Prize-winning scientists, James Watson and Francis Crick. In one fell swoop, they created the science of molecular biology – the basis of biotechnology today.

DNA exists in every cell of every living being. It is the architect of life itself, the blueprint for everything we are. Consisting of two intertwined "corkscrews," joined by a combination of four different chemical bases – Guanine, Cytosine, Adenine and Thymine, abbreviated to C, A, T and G – DNA is nothing more than a highly efficient information storage device for information about living things.

We might compare the information stored in DNA to the information stored on computer software, except that the content is significantly more profound. It is the equivalent of the computer software knowing everything about the architecture of the computer, as well as knowing how to reproduce itself.

> All living things, including our bodies, have the equivalent of an operating system in each cell of their being.

This operating system determines the colour of your eyes, tells your liver how to function and how your capillary blood vessels should form.

By modifying the DNA of a living organism, we are, in effect, upgrading its software. The possibilities are mind-boggling. Using selective breeding techniques, for example, we can typically create a new strain of plant life in about

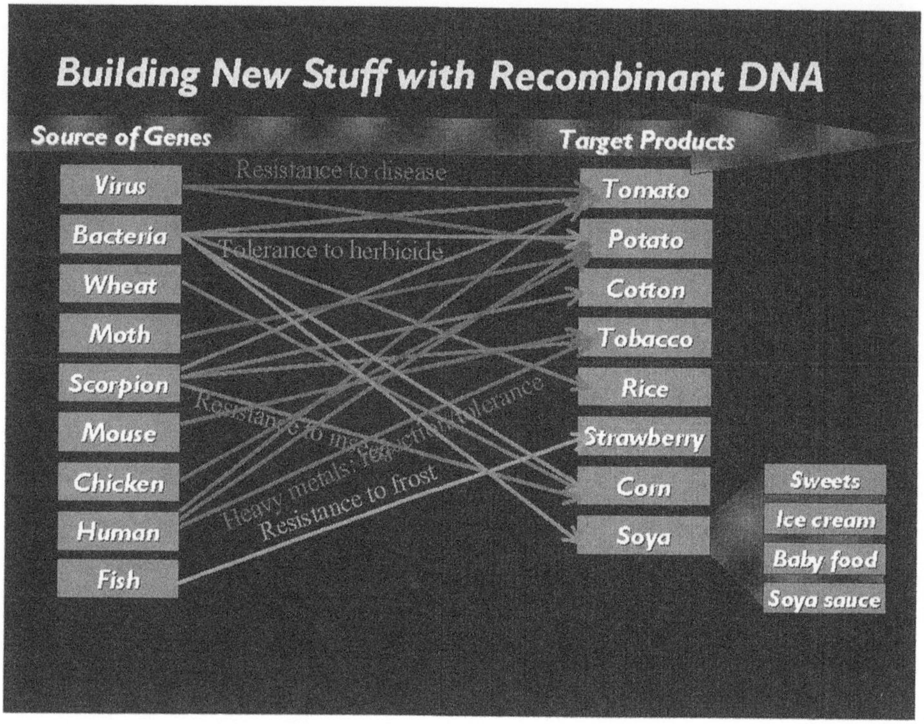
Building New Stuff with Recombinant DNA
Source of Genes
Target Products
Virus
Bacteria
Wheat
Moth
Scorpion
Mouse
Chicken
Human
Fish
Resistance to disease
Tolerance to herbicide
Resistance to frost
Tomato
Potato
Cotton
Tobacco
Rice
Strawberry
Corn
Soya
Sweets
Ice cream
Baby food
Soya sauce

eight years. Using direct genetic manipulation, we can achieve the same result in less than a day!

When we update the software of maize, we are in fact creating a new product *Maize Version 2.0*! These version numbers will prove to be very important in future. If, as is sure to happen, something is found to be harmful in a particular version of maize, then version 2.0 can simply be withdrawn from the market, and be replaced by an upgraded 2.1. Absolute identification of exactly what we are eating, for the first time!

Leaving aside the ethical concerns that may be raised by such procedures, let's look at some examples of genetic manipulation in the natural world.

- Selective breeding gives preference to certain genetic characteristics, and effectively changes the genetic code over a long period of time.
- Sunlight contains UV light, which can alter DNA bases and lead to cancer.
- AIDS is caused by HIV – a virus which adds new genetic information to cells.

In the laboratory, meanwhile, DNA manufacturing has moved well beyond the stage of theory and experimentation. It's become an everyday commercial reality. Specify the DNA you need, and a commercial DNA synthesis facility will ship you 10^{18} molecules within a day. That's 10-trillion-trillion molecules, seething inside a white blob. Yours to do with what you wish. Welcome to the new world. The world of Designer DNA!

Plastic plants and the four-legged chicken

Anyone who uses a computer will how easy it is to "cut and paste" a selection of information from one area of a document or spreadsheet to another. Imagine if you could do the same with the genes of a living organism. Newsflash: you can.

The technology is called recombinant DNA, and the possibilities are limited only by the imagination of the scientific community. You can insert genes from a virus to make a crop resistant to disease. You can insert genes from fish to make strawberries resistant to frost. You can insert genes from a scorpion to make plants resistant to insects.

It's all a question of rewiring the DNA of the target product, updating its software to build new strains that can adapt to any climate or environment. Despite the protests, it's already happening on a wide scale. In the USA, the first genetically modified crops were grown in 1996. Only four years later, they already accounted for almost 20 percent of the corn harvest, 30 percent of soy bean crop and more than 50 percent of the cotton crop.

Soon, seeds will be released to make colored cotton – blue genes for blue jeans! – without any of the toxic effects of dyes on the environment. Soon, farmers will be able to grow plants that produce plastic from fatty acids. Just think of the long-term impact on the oil companies, already hit hard by falling prices.

In the not-too-distant future, we may well be able to augment tobacco plants with the luciferase gene from fireflies, creating tobacco that glows in the dark. (You wouldn't even need to light it up.) Or we could breed petunias in any color combination, opening up a whole new field of possibility for landscape designers or flowers containing corporate logos! We could use mustard plants to harvest gold from the soil, or other plants to accumulate solar energy for later use.

And what about the animal world? Well, scientists in England have already managed to grow a chicken with four legs. It may sound like a freak of nature – but imagine what the overnight doubling of the drumstick quota could mean for chicken producers and the fast-food industry!

In California, plans have already been announced for a factory to **manufacture human skin**. It will be grown in large sheets, from fibroplast cells extracted from a **readily available source** – foreskins. **At a snip**, a single foreskin can produce more than **two football fields of dermis.**

No wonder some of us are afraid of the biotechnological future. But if these new developments prove anything, they prove just how little we really know about ourselves. And yet, we're learning. Fast.

The eyes

of the world are
turning to a
dramatic new frontier –

Inner space.

The search for the human genome

In the 1950s and 1960s, as the world's most powerful nations primed their missiles in anticipation of all-out nuclear war, a new field of battle began to conquer the popular imagination. The race for space – the last great frontier – had begun. Who would get there first? Who would fly further, faster, higher? Who would be first to set foot on the surface of the moon?

In 1957, Russia's Sputnik blazed the trail, becoming the first man-made star in the sky. In 1961, a cosmonaut named Yuri Gagarin crowned the achievement with a single orbit around the earth. Then America took the lead, with the Stars and Stripes fluttering from the Sea of Tranquillity before the decade was out.

Today, when space missions barely rate a mention on the evening news, the eyes of the world are turning to a dramatic new frontier. Inner space. As far-reaching, as challenging, as mysterious as the skies above, is the makeup of the human genome: the sequence of genes and chemical bases that contain the key to life itself.

In laboratories around the world, scientists from the USA, the UK, France and several other countries are racing to decode the genome, a project that could put every other human achievement in the shade. Never mind Mars, Everest, and the bottom of the ocean. The Human Genome Project seeks to understand and map the complexities of the ultimate alien landscape: our very own bodies.

By analyzing samples of human bodily fluid, and stripping them down to their core chemical components using specially designed parallel computers and robots, these voyagers of the future are leading the way towards the early prediction and eradication of every disease known to man.

In the shorter term, the spin-offs of genome research range from breakthroughs in molecular medicine, to more effective livestock breeding, to the

A single ounce of DNA could be 100,000 times faster than the fastest super-computer on the market today.

growing field of "DNA fingerprinting" – identifying and apprehending criminals by matching them to the unique characteristics of their DNA.

The human genome, the basic "transcript" of our DNA, is made up of a series of 100,000 genes and 3 billion chemical bases. Compare that to the 165 million bases and 25,000 genes of your average fruit-fly, and you'll see why the human genome has become the holy grail for researchers in the field. If you had to read a human genome sequence out loud, at a rate of 10 bases a second, you'd be kept busy for nine-and-a-half years. And yet, you could store the data for that sequence on a modest-sized 3-gigabyte hard drive.

As research intensifies and technology improves, the day cannot be far off when the code of the human genome – the mathematical answer to the meaning of life – is finally cracked. Already, researchers such as Craig Venter, the American scientist at the helm of Celera Genomics, have taken small but significant steps on the journey by publishing the DNA sequences of bacteria and other free-living organisms. It now appears that the elusive holy grail of biotechnology may well be reached far sooner than expected – some say as early as 2002!

Soon, as we unravel the mysteries of the double-helixes that dwell inside our cells, we will be able to shed a dazzling new light on the ancient philosopher's injunction: "Know thyself." But what will we do with this newfound knowledge? Anything we choose.

By understanding the "word-for-word" structure of DNA, we will be able to find a cure for cancer, AIDS, and almost any other genetically caused disease. By fusing the principles of biotechnology with materials science, we will be able to spin spider's silk as strong as steel cables; turn insect chitin into military armor; weave fibers from corn and E.coli bacteria; and manufacture artificial muscle, biological sensors, and lighter, stronger ceramic engines.

We will use DNA computers, guided by robotic arms and driven by millions of spinning molecules in a test tube. A single ounce of DNA could be 100,000 times faster than the fastest supercomputer on the market today.

But for all the potential benefits and spin-offs of research in the wide-open field of genetics, it's hard to escape the storm of controversy that brews whenever the spotlight shifts to the process of isolating a gene, duplicating it, and allowing it to multiply in another organism. We know this better as "cloning."

Until the advent of cloned human insulin, millions of diabetics had to make do with inferior, often incompatible insulin obtained from pigs or sheep.

The very word conjures up visions of mad dictators unleashing armies of identical zombie warriors on the world, or packs of dinosaurs, reconstituted from the blood of insects embedded in amber, going on the rampage in prehistoric safari parks.

The truth is a lot more mundane.

Cloning has long been an everyday practice in the pharmaceutical industry, where human insulin genes are produced in large vats, in a process similar to the brewing of beer. Until the advent of cloned human insulin, millions of diabetics had to make do with inferior, often incompatible insulin obtained from pigs or sheep.

And speaking of sheep... ever heard of a ewe called Dolly? Of course you have. The world's most famous wool-bearing mammal was born – or more accurately, "created" – at a research institute in Roslin, Scotland, in 1996. Through what is now known as the "Roslin Technique," a cell was extracted from an adult ewe, and put next to an unfertilized egg cell that had had its nucleus removed.

Under the influence of an electrical discharge, the donor cell was effectively encouraged to behave like a normal embryo. The "embryo" was then implanted into a surrogate mother, and Dolly the sheep was born naturally. "Dolly was created without sex, without sperm, without fertilization," explained Professor Ian Wilmut of the Roslin Institute. "She has only one natural parent... an adult ewe from which she was cloned. It's something that was never believed possible."

Since we are mammals too, Dolly has forever changed our perception of the future role of man in the reproductive process. The implications are mind-boggling, and they raise a hornet's nest of legal, moral, ethical, and spiritual concerns. Not surprisingly, many countries have placed an outright ban on experimentation in the field of human cloning. But there's no holding back the future.

Genetic engineering is the science of the **21st century** and could turn out to be one of the most **spectacular bull-runs** in history.

Genetic engineering, in whatever form it takes, is the science of the 21st century. And already, it's proving to be the foundation for what could turn out to be one of the most spectacular bull-runs in history.

Buy, buy, buy, cell, cell, cell: the birth of the new Bioeconomy

In January 1998, an American company called Geron, specializing in the development of products to combat cancer and several age-related diseases, issued a press statement that seemed to challenge one of the fundamental assertions of life as we know it.

Outlining the result of a series of experiments on the fusion of protein components with human cells, the company reported: "Three different types of cells were observed to substantially pass their normal limits of replicative life-span. These cells are continuing to grow and may be immortal."

Geron had discovered the gene that causes and controls ageing. Telomere. Overnight, the company's share price trebled. Had the company stumbled upon a way of conquering mankind's oldest fear? Would the youth of tomorrow be able to stay forever young? Alas, no.

Despite their intimations of immortality, telomeres are really the "clock genes" found at the end of each strand of DNA. They act as an indicator of the number of times a cell can divide and renew itself. Speed up the production of telomeres in an organism, by adding an enzyme called telomerase, and you can extend the life-span of humans, pets and plants. That's the theory, anyway.

In practice, Geron's discovery has far-reaching applications that range from the treatment of skin disorders to new and more effective ways of fighting arthritis and osteoporosis. But as Geron cautions, there is no evidence that the breakthrough "will translate into an extension of the maximum human life-span, which is now believed to be about 120 years."

Perhaps more significant, at least in the short term, was Geron's later announcement that they had been able to derive human embryonic stem cells for the first time in history. Stem cells are able to develop into any of the body's cell and tissue types. Mastering this technology could lead to tissue factories that would build organs, bone marrow and nerve cells on demand.

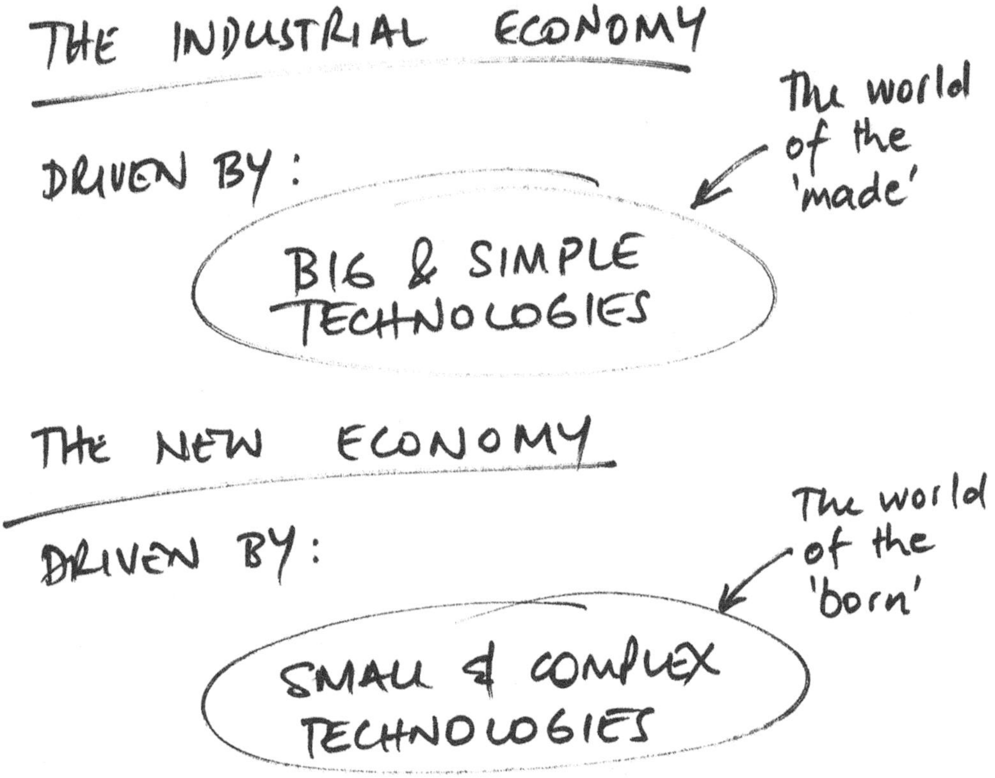
THE INDUSTRIAL ECONOMY
DRIVEN BY:
BIG & SIMPLE TECHNOLOGIES
The world of the 'made'
THE NEW ECONOMY
DRIVEN BY:
SMALL & COMPLEX TECHNOLOGIES
The world of the 'born'

Such discoveries herald a revolution in man's treatment of life-threatening diseases. But the implications stretch far beyond the field of medicine. The real, lasting impact will be felt in an arena that is already changing every aspect of the way we live our lives. The global economy. Welcome to the Second Information Revolution. Welcome to the age... of Biotechnology.

Imagine a world where the skills, infrastructure, and systems of the Information Age are fused with the complex, natural world of biology. A world where the developing sciences of miniaturization, genome research and nanotechnology would set the scene for the creation of whole new genres of life: crops, drugs, synthetic materials.

The social and economic paradigm would shift forever. The arc of the Information Economy, as spectacular as a comet streaking across the sky, would dim and fade in comparison to the rise and rise of the New Bioeconomy. We would have to radically change our thinking. The days of "Big and Simple" technologies would disappear; in their place, the new age of "Small and Complex."

From big and simple to small and complex

Think about the Industrial Revolution. What do you see? Aside from the sight of dozens of workers performing menial, repetitive tasks on a production line, the lingering image is likely to be that of a giant steam turbine, or a series of tall pillars belching smoke into the sky.

Dirty but impressive, in a monstrous sort of way, the workshops and factories of the Industrial Economy were deliberately designed to be big and simple. Even the first computers followed this principle.

ENIAC, the world's first electronic computer, commissioned in 1947, was so large that you could literally walk around inside it. Today this simple beast can be condensed onto a single silicon chip, 10 million times over.

The future has a **sneaky way of confounding** our most cherished expectations.

Today's top scientists are more likely to be working with molecules and atoms. Their world has been reduced to elements so small, they can't see them without the help of powerful computers. As technology becomes increasingly small and ever more complex, the focus is shifting into the microcosm: the fascinating world of living, organic matter.

The factories of tomorrow are more likely to be inside a test tube or on top of a laboratory workbench. What are the implications for the economy of today? For one thing, the high tech industries which now seem to absorb all the skills we can create, will start shedding jobs as programming and systems development become increasingly efficient and automated. The economy of the early 21st century will be driven by the same kind of thinking that radically transformed the auto industry in the 1970s and 1980s.

By 2010, as the Information Economy enters the fourth quarter of its lifecycle, it will begin to exhibit the same kind of pressures we are experiencing in the Industrial Economy today. Prices of raw materials and consumer goods will plummet, jobs will be shed, large corporations in fields such as software and telecommunication will be forced to consolidate.

For now, as the hot companies of the Information Economy enjoy an unprecedented boom, it's easy to believe we are not going to be affected by the typical economic growth cycle. "This time," we cry, "it's going to be different!"

Well, maybe it will be. The future has a sneaky way of confounding our most cherished expectations. But just in case, let's take a quick look at some of the underlying principles of the new economic paradigm:

- **Economies don't disappear. They build on each other.** As the industrial economy enters its fourth quarter, we won't produce less industrial products – we'll continue to produce more and more, at lower and lower prices. But the "falling price boom" will make it increasingly difficult for the old Blue Chips to be profitable. They'll decline in economic value, even as industrial outputs increase. It'll become more and more difficult for them to stay in business.

- **Technology sectors merge and build on each other to create new markets.** Example: the fusion of Information Age automation with Industrial Age manufacturing.
- **Information and knowledge become ubiquitous in the fourth quarter of an economy.** Everyone knows everything, nothing's a competitive secret anymore. While this redoubles competitiveness, it proliferates innovation and accelerates implementation of new products and services.

The Bioeconomy may well turn out to be more powerful than the Information Economy ever was! In fact, it may turn out to be the second information revolution. This new biological revolution is no longer being driven by biologists but by new age information professionals who are exploring and conquering the complexities of life!

It's not too difficult to find working examples of the trend towards "small and complex" technologies. Look at medicine, which has moved from grand, spectacular invasions of the human body to small, non-invasive operations with increasingly tiny tools, some too small for surgeons to use themselves.

We're seeing scalpels, etched from wafers of silicon, that are ten times sharper than traditional instruments. We're seeing greater use of ultrasonics which create extremely fast sonic vibrations to break up tissue without tearing or pain.

The doctor's internal intrusions are now commonly guided by tiny cameras, with their images displayed on several monitors. Doctors are already separated from their patients in this virtual environment. They may as well be countries apart, perhaps even linked via the Internet.

5

Business unusual

The explosion of fractal networks

“Every single organism on this planet,
from a bacterium to a salamander to an elephant,
has a life-cycle of its own. So do we.
At any given moment, millions of us are being
hatched, matched, or dispatched
as we move our way from one point on the cycle
to another.”

Because economies, businesses and organizations are made up of individuals, they, too, have life-cycles of their own. They're not unlike living organisms, driven by different forces at different stages of their lives.

The beginning of an organization's life-cycle is characterized by rapid, often chaotic growth, as new ideas, new products and new value propositions chase new customers. At this stage, the customer and the markets dictate everything the business does: it's driven directly by the market. Products and services are differentiated by clear customer value. Customer information is crucial.

If it succeeds, the business then enters a cycle of rapid expansion, during which rules are made up on the fly and the organization struggles to keep pace with its own growth. There are usually no staff functions such as HR – there's just no time for them. These only emerge as the business enters the second half of its life-cycle, as markets become saturated and business volumes level off.

As growth slows down, the staff departments come into a power of their own. Rules are formalized, fixed procedures established, company operating manuals written and adhered to. As an industry matures and products and services become commoditized, price becomes the only differentiator.

This creates very different organizational pressures: costs and efficiency

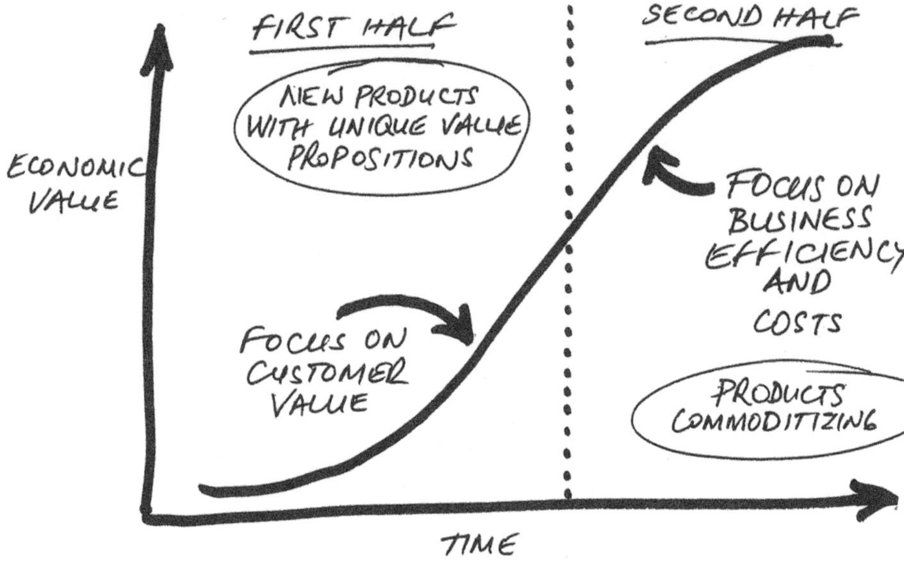
FIRST HALF
SECOND HALF
NEW PRODUCTS WITH UNIQUE VALUE PROPOSITIONS
ECONOMIC VALUE
FOCUS ON BUSINESS EFFICIENCY AND COSTS
FOCUS ON CUSTOMER VALUE
PRODUCTS COMMODITIZING
TIME

become the drivers of the business, and the financial functions rule the roost. Power shifts increasingly to middle management structures, whose purpose is to serve the organization, not the customer. The business begins turning its focus inward.

Eventually, in the fourth quarter of the business life-cycle, the annual organizational restructuring becomes an event of extreme strategic importance. A question of survival itself.

Has your organization become more important than your business?

It's at this point that the organization begins to notice fresh young competitors emerging on the periphery of its industry. Often, the organization will be at a loss to understand why its own customers are giving these new upstarts so much attention, and attaching so much credibility to what they do.

What is often forgotten is that these new companies are simply riding the second quarter of the business life-cycle. They're driven totally by customer demands... and the customers are loving it. The established fourth quarter companies will rarely take these new competitors seriously. After all, they're still pipsqueaks, and look – they're not even making any profit!

For the best examples of organizations which have become more important than their business, take a look at the banking sector.

The multiple-personality problem: Why banks just don't get it!

Let me tell you a story about my bank. I'm sure you'll reflect on your own experiences with banks as you read this – after all, we are all customers of banks and many of us have exactly the same experiences. The name of *The Bank* has been omitted to protect *The Guilty*.

As an individual, I have had a personal account with my bank for as long as I can remember. Way back in time I remember applying for my first credit card and wondering about the lengthy application form. Why was the bank asking me to fill in my name, address and bank account details when I had already been a customer at that very same branch for more than five years? I let it go because it was apparently a necessary evil on the path to getting the credit card.

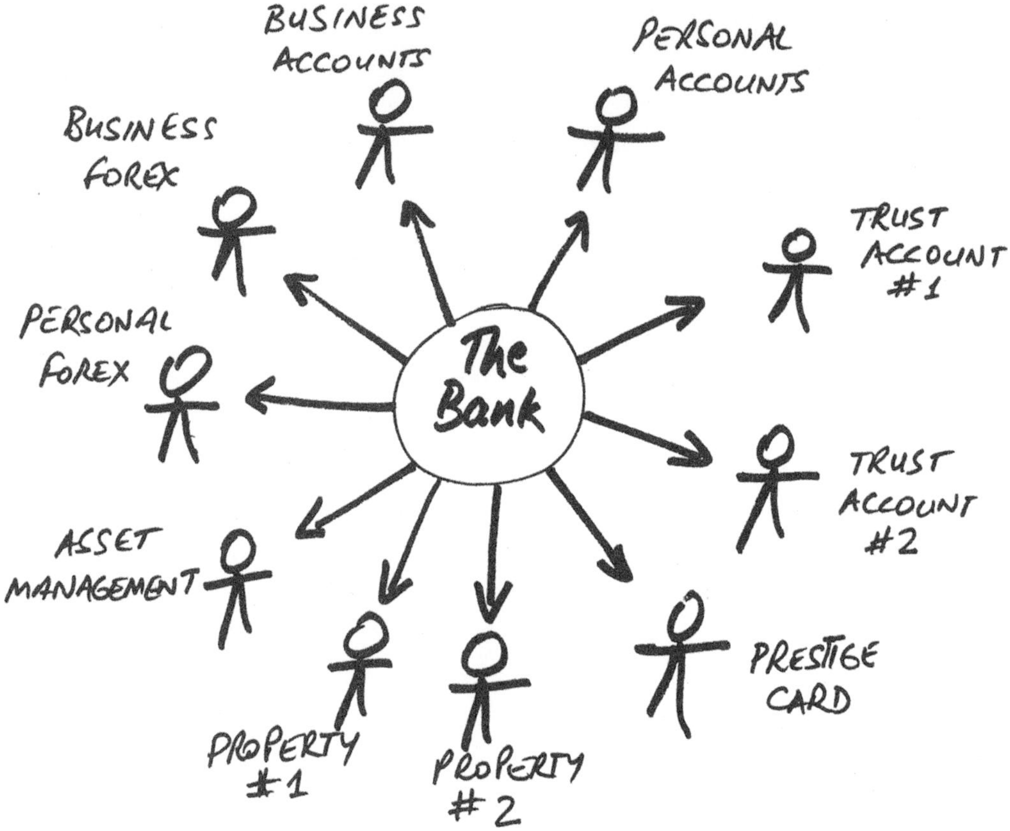

BUSINESS ACCOUNTS
PERSONAL ACCOUNTS
BUSINESS FOREX
TRUST ACCOUNT #1
PERSONAL FOREX
The Bank
TRUST ACCOUNT #2
ASSET MANAGEMENT
PRESTIGE CARD
PROPERTY #1
PROPERTY #2

With hindsight, it is absolutely clear that the *Card Division* was a totally separate entity to the *Retail Banking Division*, each with a separate organizational hierarchy and separate customer databases. At the top of each division sat an executive who would defend the autonomy of his patch to the death.

Some years later I started my first business. At the time, I dealt with a wonderful manager in my local branch office. I approached her for a business bank account. Alas, I found I couldn't deal with the same person. I had to use someone representing the *Business Banking Division*, set up "to give you, the customer, improved service levels." Again the same myriad of application forms, one for the current accounts, one each for each of the credit cards, again with the same probing questions: Name? Address? Bank? Branch? Branch number? They really pretended not to know me!

When I have a query on a credit card, there's one toll-free number for personal card queries and another for business card queries.

If I want to pay a foreign invoice, I have to deal with a whole new bunch of people in another branch. Each of them again want to register my personal details in their own idiosyncratic way.

If the foreign payment is not a business transaction, but a personal payment – for example for my daughter's university tuition fees in London – then I'm forced to deal with a third branch, and a fourth bunch of people, who are "specialists in this kind of transaction." Name? Bank branch? And so it goes.

For home loans it's *Home Loans Division* and another set of application forms. If I need a loan to purchase an automobile, it's the *Vehicle Finance Division*. For trust accounts there's a different set of specialists and requirements.

Overall, the only way for me to have a complete financial service is to have personal relationships with more than ten different people, many in different geographical and divisional parts of the bank.

Try remembering who's who when you're out of town and you need some urgent service. Oh, and of course there's now Internet Banking! But – you've guessed it – there's a whole new support infrastructure to deal with as well.

My bank thinks I'm ten different people!

If they compared these ten records they'd probably conclude that they're dealing with ten different people: "Wow! We have nine new customers!"

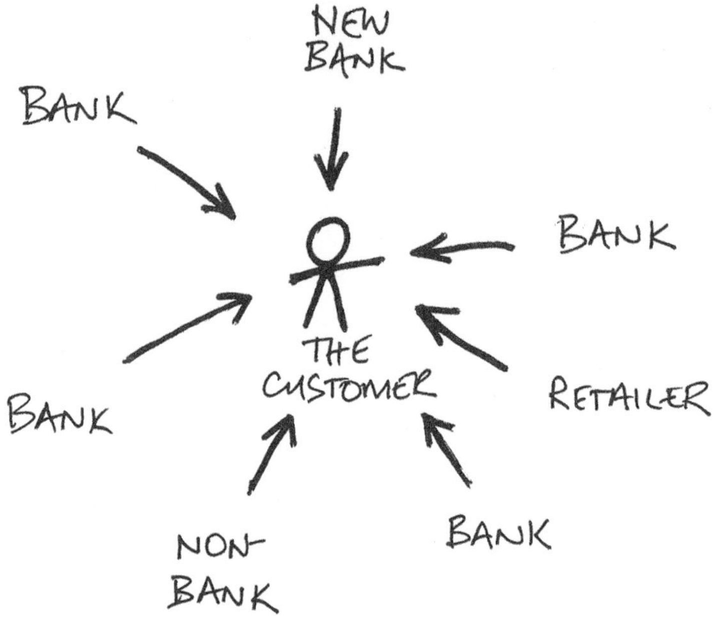
NEW BANK
BANK
BANK
BANK
THE CUSTOMER
RETAILER
NON-BANK
BANK

The bank has ten completely different sets of records on me.
Different combinations of my first and second name,
infinite varieties of my address and telephone numbers,
many at different update levels.

It's not just bad service. It's a waste of a highly valuable asset. Information. After more than ten years, my bank has amassed an enormous amount of detailed, valuable information about me, but their historic baggage of systems and organizational fiefdoms prevents them from tying it up into one picture of the individual I really am.

Recently I received an e-mail from my bank, personally addressed to "*Wolfgang Grulke.*" The e-mail started in a very promising way. *"Because you are a valued client of The Bank... we are now pleased to be able to offer you online share trading through the Asset Management Division of The Bank!"*

My spirits lifted! They know who I am!

And then it all fell apart when it came to the instructions: *"Print out the application form, complete and sign it and mail it to us."* You've guessed it! The first question was Name? closely followed by Bank? Account Number? and so on!

The routine never fails. Every new division creates a brand new record of who I am. They literally create a new "customer" every time. To change anything, even my telephone number, I have to contact every one of my ten contact points. This is in the 21st century! Banks just don't get it.

Banks don't understand that, in the *real world,*
there is only one customer, and that customer has
infinite choice – at least in a fully deregulated market!
Get that – or get out!

Banks are prime examples of organization-centred businesses, for whom life would be great if customers would only stop being such a damn nuisance.

Wherever the customer doesn't rate as #1, there is an organization that has become more important than the business!

But banks are not the only ones. They're just a convenient example we can all relate to. You can see similar organizations all around. Wherever the customer doesn't rate as #1, there is an organization that has become more important than the business!

Thankfully for the customer, things are changing.

Banks which have established their organizations, products and processes over more than a hundred years are beginning to feel serious pressure from the bright young things on their horizon.

Today, traditional banking products and services have become completely commoditized. There's no value differentiation left – one bank's check account or home loan is much like any other's. What's worse, today's big banks became that way by adding more and more products to their menu of services, each time creating a new corporate function… from *Retail Banking* to *Business Banking*, from *Asset Management* to specialized *Foreign Exchange*.

As each business grew, so did the organizational empires supporting it. The relationships between each functional line were characterized by openly hostile competitiveness. Winning the boardroom battle became the Number One priority. Information exchange was limited or non-existent. In many banks, the prestige card divisions, like American Express or Diners Club, were actively prevented from marketing their prestige products to the bank's existing retail client base.

The banks, unable to prevent their competitors from marketing prestige services to their clients, were actually preventing their own business from doing so!

This tendency for elderly organizations to protect themselves at the expense of their business is very common. And very dangerous.

The turf wars in the banking sector are partly to blame for the appalling service image banks have in the market today.

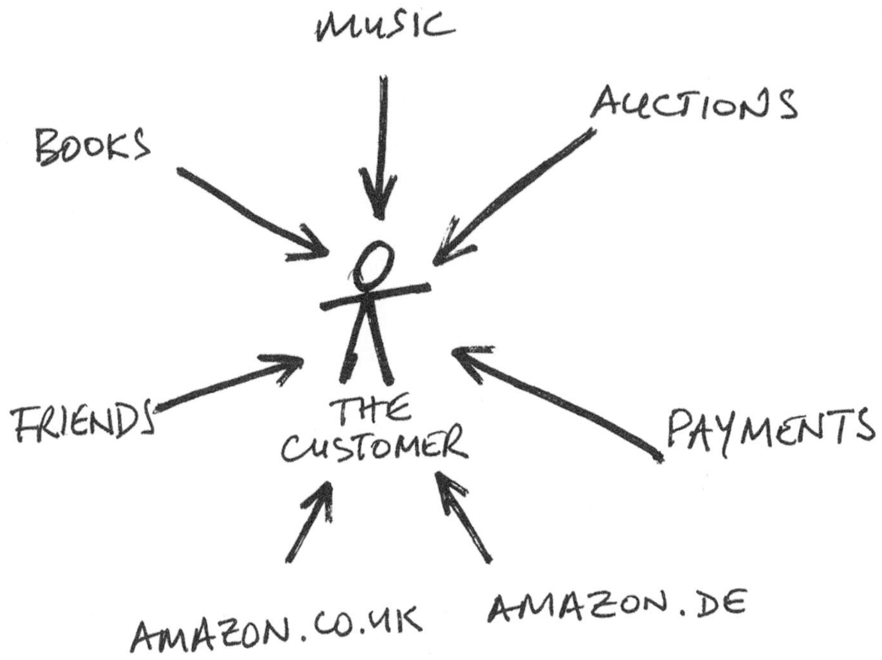
MUSIC
AUCTIONS
BOOKS
FRIENDS
THE CUSTOMER
PAYMENTS
AMAZON.CO.UK
AMAZON.DE

"Amazon can do it. So why can't the banks?"

Ever heard of Amazon.com? Of course you have. Ever ordered a book, a CD, or a movie from Amazon.com? Bid at one of their auctions? Of course you have. You and almost 20 million others! Quick to deliver, easily accessible from anywhere in the world, Amazon.com has become the classic example of the market-centered, customer-focussed business.

Way back when Amazon.com first entered our lives, we probably made the fundamental mistake of thinking they were a bookshop. We may even have thought that their key differentiator, their competitive edge, was the fact that they could deliver books more cheaply and quickly than anyone else. Not so.

Amazon's key differentiator is the information they have on their customers, and the way they capitalize on that information. With almost 20 million customers in their database, and new customers being added at a rate of almost a million a month, it's worth pointing out that 70 percent of Amazon's business comes from repeat customers. That's incredible loyalty in a fickle retail market.

At every opportunity, Amazon.com demonstrates their ability to use information as and when they need it. In fact, they have the information available before they even need it. From the "Hello, Wolfgang Grulke" I get when I visit their homepage, to the list of recommendations based on my previous purchases, this company realizes that information is the most valuable corporate asset they have. When they say "Hello, Wolfgang Grulke" they really mean it! They know it's *me*! They use every bit of information they have about me at every point of contact to add value to the process of being an Amazon customer!

When I look at a book on fossils, for instance, they may remind me that a fossil is currently being auctioned on the auction part of their site. With one click, I'll be connected to a seller somewhere else in the world, ready to make a bid.

During the past few years, I've made a habit of sending my friends around the world a little something from Amazon.com. Because of this, they now know exactly who my friends are, where they live, what they read, and so on. They present this information so well, that I've started using their database of my friends' addresses for my own purposes. After all, it's available to me wherever I am in the world, and it's always up to date.

Amazon is the classic new economy business:

- Market-centered
- Customer-focussed
- Information-rich

Best of all, Amazon.com knows something the banks don't.

Amazon knows there's only one of me!

Every bit of information I give them about myself is used to add so much value to the Amazon.com experience, that I'm quite ready to give them more information to be used in the same spirit. After all, they guarantee that they'll protect my privacy. Should they break that promise once, they'll lose a customer for good.

Doesn't it strike you as strange that while Amazon.com has licked the information problem, banks, with the biggest IT budgets in the world, can't do the same?

The secret is in their starting-points. If you start with a heap of organizational baggage and a century of business success behind you, you simply don't have the urgency or the hunger to change or improve. Why encourage existing customers to move from an existing service to a lower-cost Internet-based solution, which will probably be less profitable for the bank? Why not wait till the market forces you to do so?

Answer: because it's already too late.
The new economy tsunami waits for no one.

Banking is just one of the major Industrial Economy industries that is facing its bifurcation point. Ahead is sudden and violent turbulence. First it seems that nothing is changing, then everything changes at once. This is the reality of chaos theory in ageing industries.

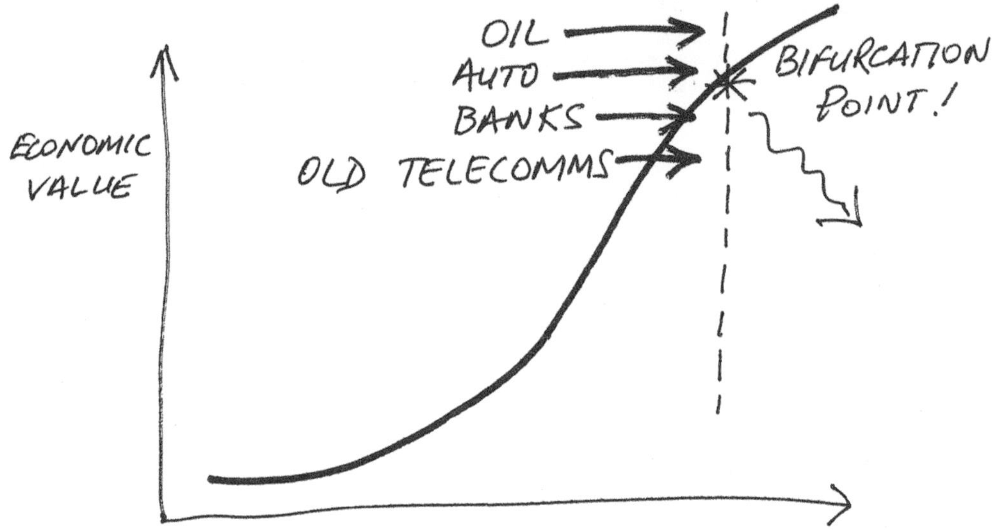
OIL
AUTO
BANKS
OLD TELECOMMS
ECONOMIC VALUE
BIFURCATION POINT!

Half of all the world's oil companies have disappeared in mergers during the past few years. There may only be four or five automobile companies in the world within five years. The world's largest banks have been created through massive mergers.

Each industry may reach its bifurcation point at a different time. But the effects are always sudden and predictable – massive mergers, dramatic investments in technology and networks, increased efficiencies, huge job losses and lower prices to consumers.

Unless you are prepared to cannibalize your own business, before your competitors force you to, you can take it as a given that you will steadily lose your customers to the new players. Your clients – the ones who've been with you for 20 years – will simply cut you out of the loop.

Forget about the competition – eat yourself!

As Amazon.com grows to dominate retail, it will offer its own banking services to cut the credit card companies out of the loop, and reduce transaction costs. That's right: a bookshop will take your bank's business. Most banks have yet to react – "We don't want to be in those markets! They're losing money!" – even while they're shedding customers and business by the day.

At the offices of an information technology company near my home, there is a Coke vending machine in the foyer. Nothing unusual about that – except for the fact that you don't need cash or a credit card to quench your thirst. You can buy a drink using nothing but your cellphone, with the cost added to your cellphone account as your cold Coke rattles down the chute into your hand.

That should give every bank CEO a chill.

Perhaps, for large established businesses it is really too late to change. It may be too expensive and slow to rebuild the organizational ark in the face of the coming competitive tsunami! Starting again may be the only option. Small nimble companies staffed by agile wizards with attitude.

Get fit! Build surfboards! Get ready to cannibalize your own business.

Even in these days of changing technologies, shifting paradigms, and radically different ground rules, it's the business basics that keep successful companies in business. As highlighted by *Fortune* magazine, these are the Seven Principles for staying ahead of the game.

1. Never be late!	5. Create a culture!
2. Don't over-promise!	6. Learn from mistakes!
3. Sweat the small stuff!	7. Shape the story!
4. Build a fortress!	

Simple, aren't they? It's been the same old story since the dawn of business science. Even Henry Ford knew and abided by those rules. So what's changed?

The context of business has changed!

Today there are **no more** local markets.
Openness and technology have created **radical new markets**,
and these *old* **rules** must now be implemented in a *new* **context**.
If you don't "get" the new context then perhaps it's **too late for a wake-up call.** You and your business **may already be dead.**

Despite the cozy familiarity of some of the above terms, they hold some rather ruthless lessons for the business leaders of today.

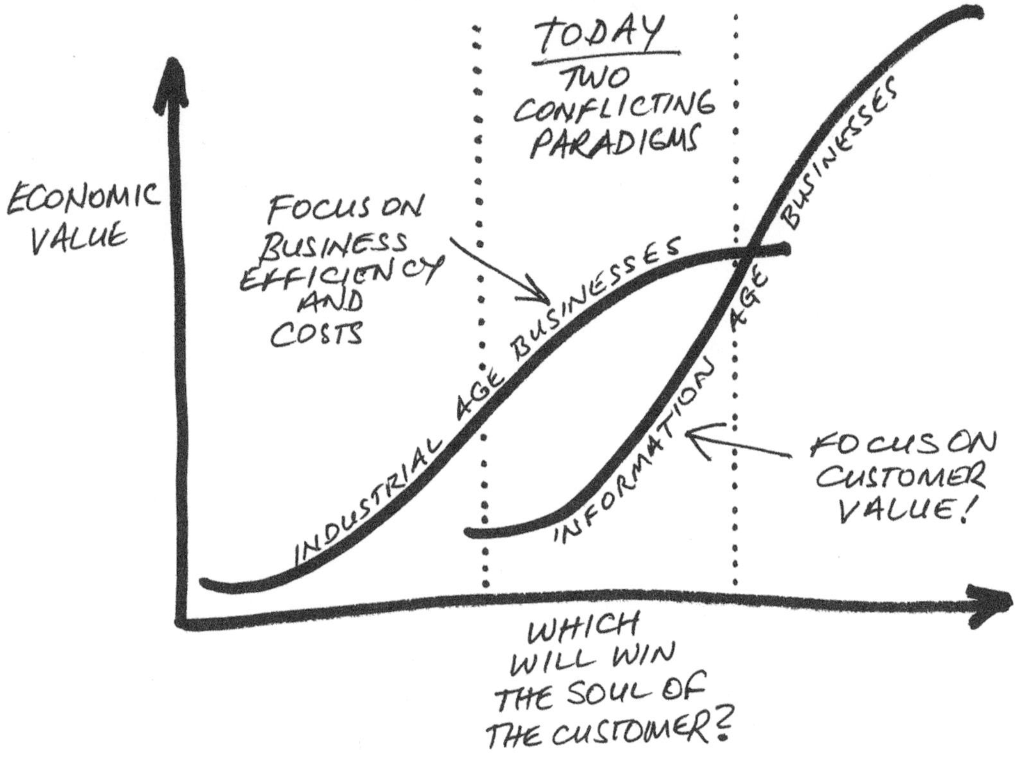
TODAY
TWO CONFLICTING PARADIGMS
ECONOMIC VALUE
FOCUS ON BUSINESS EFFICIENCY AND COSTS
INDUSTRIAL AGE BUSINESSES
INFORMATION AGE BUSINESSES
FOCUS ON CUSTOMER VALUE!
WHICH WILL WIN THE SOUL OF THE CUSTOMER?

Take the concept of learning from your mistakes. You can only learn if you *are* making mistakes. If you are part of an Industrial Age business in which the bureaucratic belts and braces prohibit people from taking real risks and making real mistakes, then you can't possibly be learning!

One of the key properties of these criteria for success is the concept of self-cannibalization. Leaders do not wait for their competition to eat their existing customers. They themselves set out to create their own "worst nightmare" by building radical new competitors outside their traditional organizations. By doing this, they escape the "innovative inertia" so common in large organizations.

For a classic case of self-cannibalization in business, take a look at BankOne, the US financial services giant. "I've spent 15 years merging more than 100 banks into BankOne," said John McCoy, the company's CEO. "I'm not ready to sit here and let somebody else take my business!" He then created a new bank under a new brand name, Wingspan Bank, to fully exploit the market opportunities of the new economy, without falling foul of the traditional historic baggage. The new company has carte blanche to destroy BankOne's business!

In the new millennium, the business revolution that started in the 1980s will continue unabated, as companies create fractal business networks to replace the traditional value chains.

Existing organizations will have to transform the fabric of their existing products, services and organizations. This will require great leadership and courage in the face of relentless change, the inertia of historic baggage, and the low likelihood of success. But one thing's for sure. If you don't take those risks, your business is guaranteed to fail.

Market power moves to the periphery

Market power, once reserved for governments and very large manufacturers, has moved to the delivery channels, the agents and retailers, during the past

few decades. Today we're seeing another dramatic shift, as market power moves inexorably to the individual consumer.

Wherever you look, the barriers to entry are being eroded. Most of the new competitors will come from outside your industry, moving the traditional goalposts and establishing new norms for service, quality and speed. Many will establish new consumer windows into a world of products and services – new interfaces for the emerging smart consumers.

Examples? CD-Now, Amazon.com, E*Trade. Other established companies, such as Federal Express, Wells Fargo Bank and American Airlines, are radically redefining their market interfaces, cutting costs and improving service as the new information infrastructures get put into place.

Brands at Internet speed

Brands have become the subliminal icons that attract consumer bees to commercial honey. Brand icons such as Virgin, Federal Express and AT&T are being used as front-ends for a range of products and services that may fall far outside the scope of the original business.

With global information networks and global consumers, more and more companies are under pressure to move from national to global brands. No time to develop your own? No problem. Buy a global brand while it's still affordable.

In the world of the Internet, it's possible to build a global brand in less than three years. In the Industrial Economy, the same process could have taken you 30 years or more.

From value chain to marketspace

The Industrial Age concept of a "value chain" is proving to be singularly unsuited to the high-speed demands of this new marketplace. There is simply no time to sit around waiting for an action to be completed by another organization or organizational function before the next action starts.

The new supply chains are increasingly displaying the characteristics of a network, with many processes happening instantly and all at once. Wherever you look, "value chains" are being replaced by "value networks." Always in

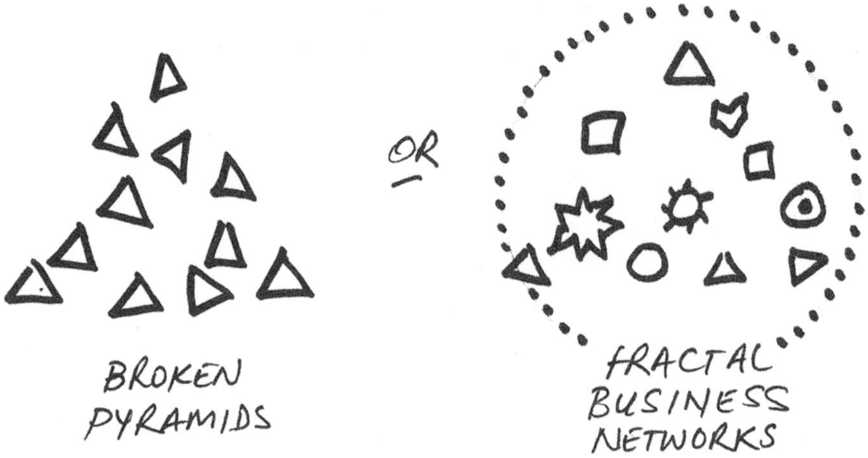
BROKEN PYRAMIDS
OR
FRACTAL BUSINESS NETWORKS

the interests of customer service, cutting time and costs, and with profound effects on management thinking and organizational style.

The Fractal Revolution

Business isn't what it used to be. Customers are changing. Services, products, entire companies, are being left behind in the rush. What used to work yesterday, won't work tomorrow. Even that very word – "work" – no longer means what it used to mean. Welcome to the new Industrial Revolution. Welcome to the Age of the Fractal Organization.

All over the world, the **Great Squeeze-Out** has begun. Traditional pyramid-shaped organizations, **built on hierarchies** of command-and-control, are **no longer effective** in fast-changing markets. **Centrally held power,** along with multiple layers of management, simply **do not translate** comfortably into great customer service.

The very understanding of the basics of good customer service has changed. Instant consumer gratification has become the norm in a world of infinite consumer choice.

The building blocks of the old organizational order are crumbling, disintegrating, creating networked "fractal" organizations. The organization as we know it… is no more.

The **Fractal** Organization is the organization of the **future.** **Flexible, adaptable, fragmented,** ultra-effective and **entirely market-focussed.** An organization that has **moved beyond** the notions of centralized control, and the **tyranny** of the Industrial Age hierarchies.

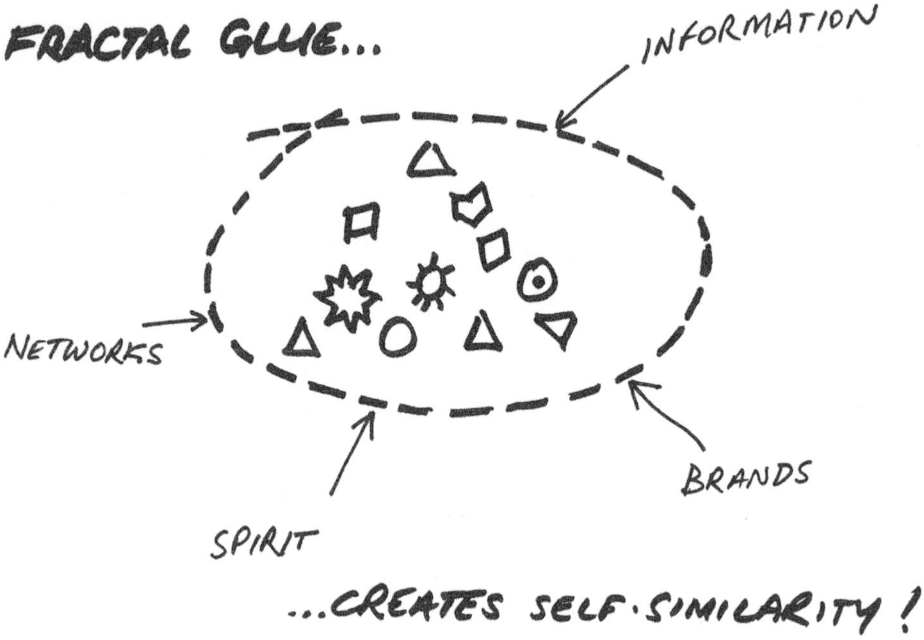
FRACTAL GLUE...
INFORMATION
NETWORKS
BRANDS
SPIRIT
...CREATES SELF-SIMILARITY!

Driven by downsized individuals, fractals live according to their own rules, interacting, connecting, feeding off each other. With access to global information networks becoming easier and cheaper by the day, small or micro business can plug in to the same resources and infrastructure as large corporations, at a fraction of the cost.

These fractal business networks are bound together by shared information, networks and brands. Shared cultures and an information-age team spirit create the self-similarity necessary to unite the fractal players in the network. This is the "fractal glue" that creates the seamless interface to the customer.

Bigger is no longer better. Leaner is meaner. Today's new graduates are no longer seeking secure, comfortable positions in the mega-corporations. They want to grow quickly and earn big, and they know they can't achieve this the way their fathers did, by becoming Company Man. Instead, they seek out small, high-growth companies, which in turn can pick and choose from the best young brains in the market. No matter where they may be.

Within these new-age organizations, business process "re-engineering" has become business process "destruction." Organization-based business processes are no longer competitive. Networks and information technologies are replacing the traditional processes with "people-less processes."

In this complex new marketplace, industries are being transformed one by one. In the last few years, the telecommunications industry has been revolutionized. What's next? My money is on financial services.

You don't have to own the product to own the customer

The global Financial Services Industry is being radically transformed by the transition to a new global economy based on information, knowledge and ideas. At the core of this revolution is the ever-increasing market power of the individual customer.

With access to an unprecedented amount of information and choice, customers are becoming a lot smarter and more demanding. There's nowhere left for an uncompetitive business to hide. If you're not structuring your business around the new market demands, then you're probably not going to be in business for very much longer.

Customers are voting with their wallets.

In the banking sector, customers are already voting with their wallets. Banks have already lost touch with the people they're supposed to serve. A recent American study showed that only two in ten customers knew someone at their local branch by name. Do you?

Today's banks only manage around 12 percent of personal savings. These declining funds are increasingly uncovered by other investments, making risk management very difficult, if not impossible. Mortgages and home loans are the last bastion of big banking profit. But even these are now being challenged by non-banks with famous brand names, from Virgin to GM.

Banks are realizing that risk can no longer be covered by physical assets. Small businesses simply don't have them, and individuals "hide" them to optimize their personal taxes!

Today, financial services companies process less than 30 percent of all credit card transactions. Their most powerful competitors are the non-banks, professional services companies that focus on nothing else.

European banks will lose up to $65 billion per annum in currency exchange revenues per annum as a result of the implementation of the Euro. More than half of branch outlets will have been shut down by 2003.

Customer expectations of financial services players have changed fundamentally. In this turbulent market, Bankers Trust was one of the first "banks" that attempted to identify those financial services that would not change. In future, they believe, financial services will be bought by customers according to "five unchanging financial services functions."

Unchanging Financial Services Functions
Financing
Risk management
Trading and positioning
Advising
Transaction processing

We are moving from the concept of a *client* and a *customer* to the anarchy of smart consumers.

Increasingly banks are having to compete with players from outside the traditional industry for these markets. For example, they've already lost the transaction processing segment. Interestingly, only one of the five functions, Advising, involves direct and intimate customer relationships. This will become the high-ground of financial services.

Within five years, the traditional concept of "a bank," "an insurer" and "a broker" will have all but disappeared. The dominant competitors will be new mega-players who have understood this fundamental shift in customer expectations. Their market focus will be based on the "five unchanging financial services functions," rather than the traditional channel structures. They will have new value propositions, entirely appropriate for the new kind of customer: The Smart Consumer.

But when will all this happen? Regulators and Industry associations will try to slow down the process, allegedly to "protect the consumer," but really in order to protect their own dying services and markets.

Who will succeed? Easy. Those companies that start behaving as if this open, deregulated future, the age of the Smart Consumer, has already arrived. If history is anything to go by, the winners will not be the current leaders in the financial services industry. The real winners will be new, nimble players, armed with great ideas and little historic baggage to hold them back.

Today you can buy a full range of financial services from non-financial services companies, all the way from British Airways to GM to AT&T to Volkswagen. Technology is leading these companies into the 21st century. Technology is defining their business strategy.

If you're an existing financial services player, your challenge is to build on your legacy while competing head-on with radical new competitors.

Here's the biggest lesson of them all. If you want to succeed, you no longer have to own the product that you sell. What you do have to own, is the customer relationship. For agents and brokers, this will come as no surprise. For those who run the factories, it'll sound like heresy.

Today,

businesses are defined more by

their relationships than by their products!

The whole economic pie

is up for grabs.

Competition for the customer

will be fierce,

unparalleled and

radically different.

So what does all this mean to you?

You may not work in the IT, telecommunications, or financial services industries. You may be wondering what any of this has to do with you. The answer is simple. Plenty. Whoever you are, whatever you do, think about the future of your business in the following terms.

• The transformation of the value chain into a value network.
• The decline in importance of raw materials and the physical content of products.
• The changing nature in the value of customer information and who is best positioned to exploit it.
• From YOUR position in YOUR industry, how will these drivers affect you?
• What are the opportunities that the new economy presents to you?
• What is your worst nightmare in terms of future competitors?
• What will create your industry's bifurcation point?

For *your* future business positioning you have to choose from two equally viable extremes. You may choose to be a highly *visible consumer window* into a world of products and services. Or you may choose to be a *high-quality, low-cost producer* of niche products or services, sold through someone else's window or brand. You may even choose to be both.

In each area, competition for the customer will be fierce, unparalleled and radically different. Change truly is the only constant. Your industry is no different. Global markets are in turmoil. The whole economic pie is up for grabs. Opportunities are everywhere, available to everyone.

For those who understand the new rules, for the competitively fit and nimble, for those who are unafraid to think ahead and innovate, this truly is a world of boundless opportunity.

TRADITIONAL OFFICE/FACTORY JOBS
NON-TRADITIONAL/FRACTAL JOBS
1970s
TODAY
2020s
TOURISM
PERSONAL FINANCIAL SERVICES
HEALTH CARE
ENTREPRENEUR
HIGH TECH
GENERAL SERVICES

So where have all the jobs gone?

With all this radical transformation in the workplace and the marketplace, it's fair to wonder what will happen to the jobs that drive today's economy.

Even today, almost half the jobs in the developed world are no longer found in the traditional factory or office environment. The SOHO environment – Small Office Home Office – has become the environment of choice for most professional and knowledge workers.

During the next 20 years, nearly all new jobs that will be created will be outside the traditional workplace. In the USA today, only 35 percent of employees work the 9-to-5 workday. What was once the exception is fast becoming the norm.

As corporates get bigger in terms of revenues and market power, smaller in terms of number of direct employees, and increasingly networked, with outsourced functions, business partners and suppliers, they will become true fractal business networks, with each fractal completely geared to customers and markets.

The "corporate job," so sought after in the Industrial Economy, is no longer the goal of the top business school graduates. They seek to become part of exploding fractal businesses, hoping to reach financial maturity in their 30s, and not after retirement. They seek multiple concurrent careers, not one long, dragged-out career.

The major careers of the 2020s will be in the high-technology and services industries, in leisure, tourism and education. The most sought-after characteristics will be entrepreneurship, flexibility, risk-taking and innovation. How do you rank yourself personally against these? How do others see you? What is your current personal "market cap" when ranked against these? Could you improve your personal market value?

In the new fractal job market of the future, a new set of competencies will determine success.

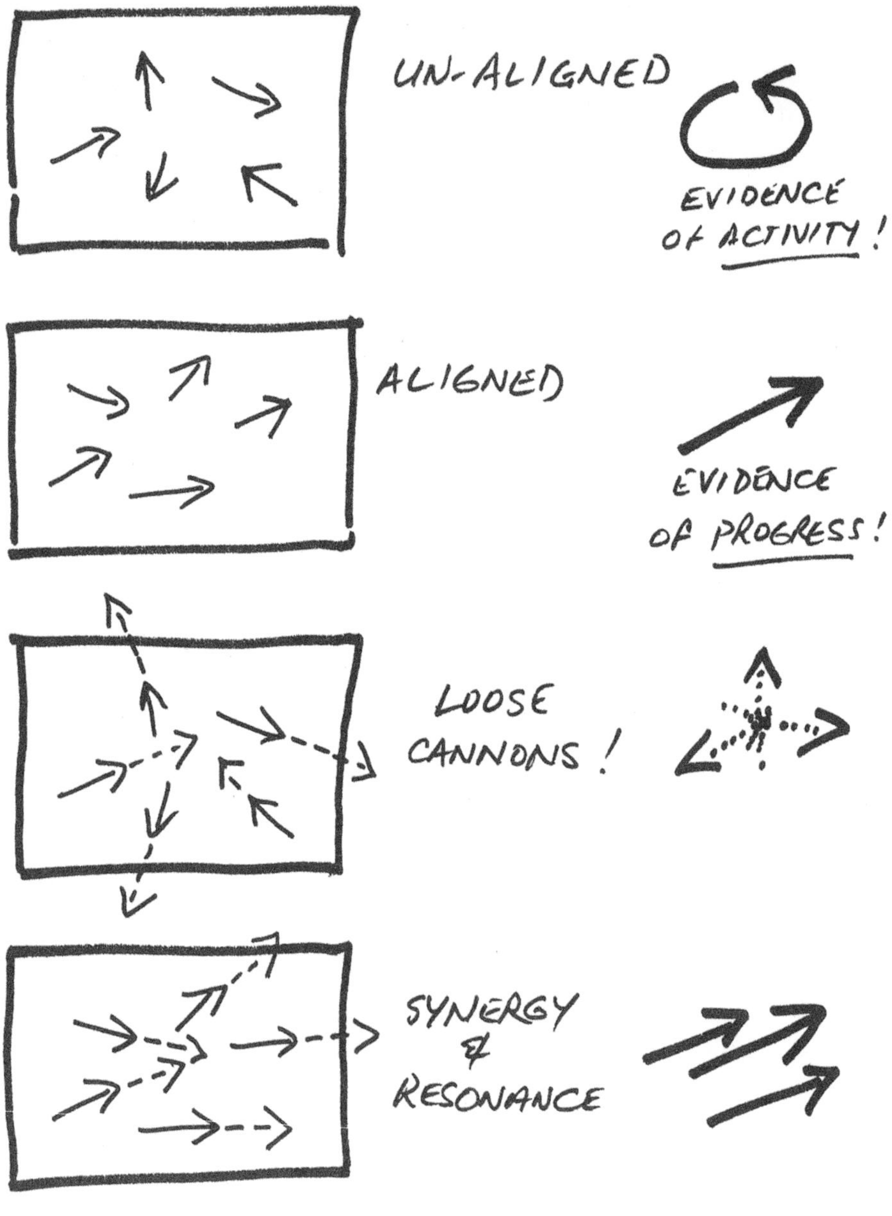
UN-ALIGNED
EVIDENCE
OF ACTIVITY!
ALIGNED
EVIDENCE
OF PROGRESS!
LOOSE
CANNONS!
SYNERGY
&
RESONANCE

Industrial Age	Information Age
Knowledge	Skills
Experience	Attitude
Management	Leadership

The new jobs demand the ability to apply knowledge in the form of skills. Experience has continually less value as the pace of change increases – only the right attitude to un-learn at every step of the way will win the day. In a fractal business network there are fewer management jobs and greater demand for leadership at all levels.

Today, construction companies and builders are reporting exploding demands for home offices and studies, almost unheard of earlier in the 1900s except for the very rich. At the center of this new work-style and lifestyle is the ubiquitous computer.

As soon as the PC arrives in the home, one bedroom stops being a bedroom and begins its transformation into a study or workspace. In fact, every room in the house becomes a multi-purpose room. The loft, the space under the stairs, the spare bedroom: all are targets for this new obsession. It's forever changing the way we work, learn and live. Work isn't where you go. It's what you do.

The same goes for learning. Universities and schools will be last to understand, as their students migrate to other countries and continents to study. There'll be an invisible, electronic migration to best-of-breed learning – wherever in the world it may be.

Alignment and empowerment: Never confuse activity with progress!

Once you're in an organization, it will become immediately clear if the individuals in it are aligned around a common purpose. Certainly the customers will be able to tell!

Organizational textbooks will tell you that organizational synergy is only created once you empower staff. The trouble is that if you empower an un-aligned organization you don't get synergy – you get loose cannons! The customer never quite knows what to expect wherever he or she touches the organization.

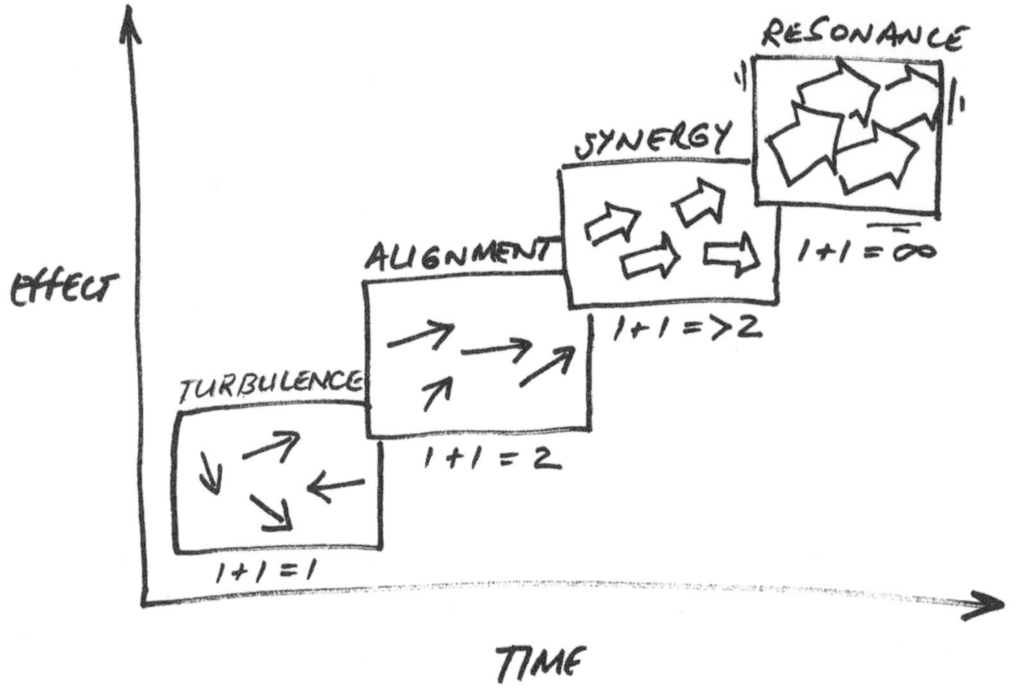
RESONANCE
SYNERGY
ALIGNMENT
EFFECT
TURBULENCE
1+1=∞
1+1=>2
1+1=2
1+1=1
TIME

Why look for synergy when you can resonate?

Tacoma, Washington State, 1947. One of the world's longest suspension bridges crosses a steep wooded ravine. A soft breeze blows along the valley and starts resonating with the bridge structure. A slight vibration starts.

For days, the soft breeze continues unabated. Eventually the bridge is twisting as if in violent storm. Except you can't even feel the breeze. The bridge becomes a tourist attraction. People from miles around drive their cars onto the swaying road surface to have their photo taken.

Then, suddenly, the bridge snaps. Huge fragments tumble into the valley below. What remains is held up precariously, as if by spiders' silk.

The Tacoma River Bridge disaster was the powerful, but negative, consequence of a force we call resonance. Listen carefully: it's all around us. It's the new goal of organizations that were once satisfied with a simple striving for synergy.

But resonance is more than just the new corporate buzzword.

It's a way of building businesses by building positive relationships. Between employees. With customers. Between levels of management. With business partners.

Peter Senge, the MIT lecturer and guru of Organizational Learning, talks a lot about "creative tension." He uses an elastic band, stretched taut between his hands, to illustrate his point. Then he brings his hands together and the elastic band hangs limp and lifeless – just like many organizations.

Whenever I have heard Peter talk about "creative tension," I have thought about "resonance."

You can sense both "creative tension" and "resonance" when you deal with some organizations as a customer. It's a real pleasure to do business with them. It's not just about "synergy," or "empowerment." It's an all-embracing passion for the business and the customer.

Resonance is created not by one or two grand gestures, but by thousands of small actions by hundreds of people, day after day. Staff can readily identify examples of behavior that resonates with a company's goals and values. The opposite of this is dissonance. Watch out for it. It can destroy an organization.

Machines
too complex to understand,
networks too
complex
to manage,
organizations too demanding
to lead,
customers too
demanding to satisfy.

The key to getting ahead in the new economy, the key to resonating, is to build powerful, vibrant relationships inside and outside your company, between your company, your customers and your partners.

Is there no end in sight for the digital economy?

The Industrial Economy has been part of our lives for the last 250 years. Before that, the Agricultural Economy dominated the landscape for thousands of years. The Information Economy, on the other hand, is just a few decades old… and already it's about to be trampled in the rush to build the New Bioeconomy.

No wonder some of us are scared. No wonder some of us are hesitant. No wonder some of us are asking: does this mean that the next economy will last only a few weeks or months? Talk about Future Shock!

But it now seems that something even more dramatic and fundamental has been going on for the past 30 to 40 years. A quantum change in the complexity of everything around us, creating shock wave upon shock wave as we gird ourselves for the challenges and opportunities of the future.

A quantum change in the nature of complexity

"Machines too complex to understand; networks too complex to manage; organizations too demanding to lead; customers too demanding to satisfy."

Recognize it? It's the familiar lament of the modern-day executive in every corner of the world.

Share markets, now driven by tens of millions of individuals rather than scores of large organizations, have become "too complex to predict." A large proportion of trades on the NYSE and Nasdaq are now the result of ultra-busy "day traders." The falling price of commissions for online trades has pushed trading volumes up significantly.

In some cases commissions are under $20 per trade, whereas an equivalent trade three years ago would have attracted a commission of more than $1,000. With such low commissions, there's simply no need to wait until you recoup a relatively large commission before selling.

Changes in sentiment can shift entire markets in minutes. Rational information, on the other hand, appears to take much longer to assimilate. A rumour

The power of the market lies with you and I, rather than with large organizations and central government.

about Bill Gates's health will push the Microsoft price down in an instant: "I must sell just in case it is true. If it isn't, I can always re-buy later, at a lower price." Of course, studied and measured reports about Microsoft's prospects are widely available, but it could take months for their effect to filter through to the share price.

Today's markets seem to depend more on herd behavior rather than anything else. But when we hear that kind of language, along with "swarming," "chaos," "everything happening at once," and "flocks of investors shifting course at the slightest crack of a twig," we should ask...

Is the world around us really getting out of control?

Or is the system itself simply exhibiting biological characteristics?

Towards the New Bioeconomy

It's a fact that the New Economy is being driven by consumers rather than producers. The power of the market lies with you and I, rather than with large organizations and central government.

Today, it seems, we need to embrace biological characteristics and natural systems in order to make sense of the chaos and complexity around us.

Those who don't understand the new rules will simply see the current transition as frightening and chaotic. They'll miss the good old days, and wonder why things have to be so different and confusing. But once we understand the nature of the two economic models, and we begin to see the transitional path between them, it all seems a lot less daunting.

Let's call this new economic paradigm the Bioeconomy. It will be an economy born from a fusion of molecular science and biotechnology, but it will also be an economy which requires us to embrace biological and natural systems, in business, government and in our personal lives.

But wait a second... if we're making this bold move from the Industrial Economy to the Bioeconomy, whatever happened to the Information Economy?

It was there last time you looked, wasn't it?

The Information Economy **may prove** to be **nothing more** than the beginning of a **major economic gear-shift** in which the basic **economic resources** shifted from the **tangible** to the **invisible.**

Relax. It's still there. But in years to come, we'll see it as nothing more than the beginning of a major gear-shift, profound but short-lived, in which the basic economic resources shifted from the big, simple and tangible...

Raw materials, real estate and cheap labor...

...to the small, complex and intangible: Information, knowledge, skills and ideas.

The Information Economy may turn out to have been just the first micro-cycle of a new macro-cycle. The New Bioeconomy may, in fact, prove to be another long-lasting all-pervasive economy, with a life-cycle not dissimilar to the Industrial Economy itself.

For now, let's take a deep breath and look at some of the forces that will shape the new economy. Who will be the winners? Who will be the losers? Where will you fit in?

Factors impeding the progress of the Bioeconomy

Fear of the unknown

Our instinctive fear of the unknown will inhibit us from seizing the day when it comes to putting bioeconomic thinking into action. Ethical and moral concerns will weigh heavily on our minds.

Only by taking personal responsibility for understanding the issues, and cutting through the mass of conflicting news coverage and "expert opinions," can we hope to put these fears into perspective.

In the meantime, the technological advances will race ahead of our ability to understand their implications. We'll find ourselves engaged in a constant battle between morbid curiosity and cautious engagement.

Frankenstein Foods:

Are we

playing **God**

with nature?

Ethical and moral issues

Remember the world's first test-tube baby? Well, she's not a baby anymore! In 1978, when Louise Brown was born in England, the circumstances and technology surrounding her birth were the subject of intense ethical and moral debate. But today, around the world, we accept in-vitro fertilization as a viable and routine route to childbirth for couples battling the agony of infertility.

In the same way, the current ethical and moral tangle over the merits of Genetically Modified foods is likely to cool off as these foods become part of our everyday lifestyle. Certainly, there are very real concerns and conflicts with existing religious and cultural norms: "Who are we to play God with nature?" But it's also true that much of the current anti-GM thinking is based on ill-informed and inflammatory reporting.

For example, when American BioTech firms took GM seeds to India, many reports saw it as an "invasion." Given the facts, they could just as easily have looked at it this way: "American Biotechnology firms are investing in India as part of a quest to double agricultural output on the subcontinent."

It's all a matter of perspective. The most hysterical reactions have come from the British tabloid press, with their lurid reports of activists going out in the dead of night to cut down "Frankenstein crops." Not surprisingly, many farmers have joined the bandwagon to protest against the risks of their own "natural" crops being "contaminated" by adjoining GM crops.

Are they really afraid of their crops becoming insect-resistant? Or could the possibility that their neighboring farmers might double their crop yields have anything to do with it? It's amazing how often economic fears are couched in moral terms.

And it's likely to get worse. As the line blurs between our understanding of what exactly constitutes "food" and "drugs," imagine what the media will do with a story about a cholera vaccine in bananas, or a TB vaccine in maize. Never mind the potential benefits.

Either way, the New Bioeconomy will provide us with plenty of food for thought. Each scientific advance brings with it a new set of concerns and unknowns. But here's the really scary part: we'll never know what we don't know, unless we're bold enough to find out for ourselves.

Radical and political interest groups

During our research into Biotechnology, we found this "disclaimer" at the start of one Russian university's dissertation on genetics:

GENETICS

COMMENTS BY COMRADE LYSENKO

COMRADES,

WHILE PHYSICS AND CHEMISTRY REMAIN PURE SCIENCES, GENETICS IS THE BASTARD CHILD OF THE DECADENT CAPITALIST SOCIETY

Aside from proving that some social and political viewpoints remain mired in the distant past, it's a classic example of the extreme attitudes that will hog the spotlight as the Bioeconomy goes public.

Governments will regulate more

Pushed by public debate, and sometimes by flagging popularity at the polls, governments will find it hard to resist the temptation to regulate more. Why? To protect us, of course! But beware. There is nothing more dangerous than governments being pushed to regulate what they don't understand.

Investor perceptions

As long as investors perceive biotechnology stocks as high risk, with long payback periods, the growth of the New Bioeconomy will be slower than anticipated. Unknown regulatory obstacles will add to insecurity. Can an American biotechnology firm really hope to do well if its Genetically Modified seeds are banned in Britain?

These are some of the factors that could have a negative effect on the emergent economy. Now let's take a look at the upside.

Factors driving us towards the Bioeconomy

"We're killing the planet!"

The products of the Bioeconomy represent our first real hope of manufacturing without the use of the toxic chemicals that characterize our current forms of industry. No need for harmful dyestuffs, printing inks, or insecticides. We'll also be able to distribute and access information without having to destroy a rain forest a day.

"We must find a way to feed the masses!"

Although we have already increased agricultural output by an order of magnitude over the last half-a-century, the opportunities presented by GM crops are targeted and dramatic. We could, for instance, produce 5,000 tomatoes on a single plant, or grow maize in the most arid conditions.

A cure for diseases such as AIDS and cancer

Our fear of disease will always be greater than our fear of the cures. We will always strive to go the next step – if only to save a friend or relative.

Success of Human Genome projects

As these projects mature and produce their expected results, most likely earlier than expected, we'll see feverish activity to bring products based on this new science infrastructure to market.

Consumer diversity of choice

As consumers, we are always looking for the Next Big Thing. We've grown accustomed to an ever-increasing array of choices. We'll vote for these new products with our wallets!

Economic opportunity

The Bioeconomy presents us with a multi-trillion-dollar opportunity for growth. For all the initial caution, it will attract attention and investments

The third quarter of
the New Bioeconomy **will**
belong to everyone
– new products and services
will change the way we
live and work, and the way
companies compete.

from innovators worldwide. Many of the traditional pharmaceutical companies will be obliged to participate in these new product areas as the "falling price boom" hits their traditional product lines. They'll be forced to generate a thirst for new products to stimulate consumer demand.

What's next for the New Bioeconomy?

It's still early days. But the excitement is building.

During the First Quarter of this new economy, the science companies, such as Amgen, will benefit most. Economic activity during this period will be based primarily on the marketing of basic science and technology. For the most part, the customers will be other science and technology firms.

In the Second Quarter, the infrastructure companies will start booming. Access to genome catalogs will be sold in the same way that Microsoft licenses software today. Technology platforms will become ubiquitous, as thousands of new companies enter the fields of recombinant biology, drug delivery, and so on.

The Third Quarter will belong to the rest of us. New products and services will change the way we live and work, and the way companies compete. The boom will echo the dramatic growth of the IT and telecommunications industries which occurred from the late 1980s onwards. Only this time, it'll be across a far broader front, with technology transfer at a far greater speed.

So where will investors find these promising new companies?

Pinpointing the future stars of the Bioeconomy is not as easy as it may seem. There is no BioTech sector on any stock exchange.

Some of the "older" players, who will be first to feel the pinch of the "falling price boom," can be found in the Chemical and Pharmaceutical sectors. Among them: Dow Chemical, BASF, Johnson and Johnson.

Many companies from across these sectors are merging to create "Life Sciences" companies. You'll be hearing a lot more of that buzzword over the next few years.

It's about as easy to find the future winners and losers of the Bioeconomy as it would have been to predict the winners and losers of the burgeoning computer industry in the early 1970s.

We'll also be seeing more and more IT giants, such as IBM, getting closely involved on the "information" side of complex genome projects. They too could become "boom" companies of the New Bioeconomy.

Organizations such as NASA and MIT are already having a significant impact on the advance of the new technologies. But since they're not private listed companies, there's really no telling where the benefits of their research will eventually end up.

The truth is, it's about as easy to find the future winners and losers of the Bioeconomy, as it would have been to predict the winners and losers of the burgeoning computer industry in the early 1970s. We all know what happened to Apple and Microsoft, but 90 percent of the other major players have totally disappeared, and many of today's major players did not even exist.

So it will be with the New Bioeconomy. Are you willing to take a chance?

What will the bioeconomy mean for business?

Production will be decentralized

- Small-scale manufacturing, anywhere, anytime
- Declining demand for mass transport, along with an explosion in courier services

New products to combat the "falling price boom"

- Don't build it if you can grow it
- Cheap plants that can grow anything, such as plastics from fatty acids

Old sectors will wither and die

- Bandwidth, programming, manufacturing and raw materials

The Bioeconomy may well have an extended life-cycle measured in hundreds of years.

New sectors will emerge

- Information+Biotech+materials technologies = Material Sciences
- Pharmaceutical+Biotech+healthcare=Life Sciences
- NanoManufacturing will emerge as a boom industry in the longer term

Organizations and workstyles will change

- Old companies will become larger and more efficient, primarily through mergers
- New companies will thrive on being smaller and more niched
- Fractal business clusters will predominate
- The "skilled elite" will exercise unprecedented choice and personal power

The Bioeconomy will have an extended life-cycle

- Based on the new global information infrastructure, it will be the first economy to be built entirely on knowledge and attitudes, rather than goods and services
- Copyrights and patents will no longer prove adequate business protection. Business advantage will only be gained by speed of action

What will the Bioeconomy mean for you and me?

We will all live longer and work longer

Life expectancy could double in the next 20 years. What if you don't want to live that long? Will you have the right to choose? What about the implications for insurers and pension schemes? What about the future of healthcare?

The smaller things get
the more important their
impact may become

You will have to take personal responsibility

Increasingly, in this brave new world, you will have to take personal responsibility for your position on:

- Genetic fingerprinting. Will your Bill of Rights be violated if someone obtains a sample of DNA from your hair-clippings? Who will have the right to store information about you in biological information systems? Who will have the right to see it?
- Designer organs. Human cloning. Genetically modified foodstuffs.

Make your views heard. Lobby, lobby, lobby. No-one else will do it for you!

More and more, the skills required for business success will move from the physical to the conceptual. In the Industrial Economy, "bigger" was inherently better and more impressive. In the Bioeconomy, you'll have to think small to think big. You might even have to think "invisible" if you really want to be noticed.

Remember the old saying: "You are what you eat." It's never been more true than in the New Bioeconomy.

"We are at the beginning of the revolution, rather than in the middle. Most people – most scientists – have no understanding of how powerful this technology is. Scientists are taught to do the experiments, get the data, interpret that data, and not go beyond what that data says. People assume that the future technology is basically going to be same as today's. They don't understand that the technology is exploding around us. Everything is going to be different."
Lee Silver, University of Princeton

What will the Global Economy look like in 2020?

Despite the emergence of the new Bioeconomy, all the "old" economies will still be in place. They'll build on each other as new technologies make the older economies ever more efficient.

Only 2.5 percent of the workforce will be in agriculture.

Only 2.5 percent of the workforce may be in manufacturing.

More than 50 percent of the workforce will be in services. Many of these will be brand new jobs created by new products and technologies.

Almost 50 percent of the world economy could be based on the Bioeconomy.

Yes, but what will the future REALLY be like?

It will be a future driven by the power of technology. But it will not be a future of cold gray steel.

Products will increasingly be grown rather than manufactured.

We will become increasingly dependent on interdependent systems, which will have the characteristics of living organisms.

We will build organizations around principles inherent in natural systems, rather than the central control hierarchies of the Industrial Age.

Networks and organizations will resemble complex, seemingly unsupervised ecologies.

This "individual chaos" will result in "overall harmony," realizing Adam Smith's promise of free markets for the first time, and creating opportunities for unparalleled growth and unprecedented economic access into the bargain.

The future economy will soon be upon us
like a sudden tidal wave –
a tsunami!

OR

The Bioeconomy offers the promise of life in an ideal world. What will it take to turn this promise into reality?

Quality thinking. Vision.

Energy and passion.

And more than anything else…

the ability to learn from the future!

Get ready for the big tsunami

If you have an existing successful business, built up over many years, you may no longer be able to afford the luxury of change. The historic baggage of your past success may lie so heavily on your back, that you will not be able to stare the future firmly in the face.

Your organization may be like a proverbial ark – facing a business tsunami.

You may not be nimble or determined enough to change. You may have to create a few radical new businesses that will seriously cannibalize your existing cash cows.

The new economy tsunami is coming.

What you need is to spawn independent young companies staffed by nimble young things.

Build surfboards, an ark won't do!

6

Top companies of the 2020s

Tomorrow's business giants

"The next time you read an article about computers the size of a pinhead, or the US Army synthesizing armor from insect chitin, don't discuss it with your pals in the pub. Discuss it with your stockbroker."

The world's economy has changed fundamentally with the shift from Industrial Age thinking to the global dynamics of the Information Age. More dramatic changes are still to come.

The top global companies of the 2020s

Today the world's biggest companies, by sales and profitability, are still the Industrial Age giants. But huge amounts of money are being invested and made in new and radically different sectors.

Market capitalization is the market's true measure of earning potential, and the New Economy is well represented among the biggest market caps. Right up there with GE, Exxon, Shell, Wal-Mart, AT&T and BP Amoco, are Microsoft, IBM, Intel, Nokia and Vodafone. But it's too late to invest in these companies. These companies made millionaires years ago, while we were still investing in historically important players.

In the next 20 years, the profitability of the major industrial sectors – especially raw materials and manufacturing – will gradually wither away. Powerful new sectors will emerge as the Information Economy gives way to the Bioeconomy.

The new economy of

the next 20 years

will be built on connectivity and

the expansion of the world's digital skin.

Simultaneously, with the explosion of

the availabilty of bandwidth,

prices will plummet.

Who will be the global heavyweights of the year 2020? Let's take a look for ourselves.

UN Motors

For the past three decades, the world's biggest company has been an automaker. The only way these Industrial Age giants will survive and grow, is by consolidating. UN Motors may well be a combination of the world's three big car makers – GM, Ford and DaimlerChrysler. (Editor's note: this was written in August 1999, five months before these fierce competitors created a single joint venture company through which they will do the procurement for all their parts, products and raw materials. Common systems will ease their way to eventual total integration. Only the car brands will survive as separate entities.)

NorCisc Services (incorporating A&BT&T)

The new economy of the next 20 years will be built on connectivity and the expansion of the world's digital skin. Simultaneously, with the explosion of the availability of bandwidth, prices will plummet. With this in mind, AT&T and British Telecom could join forces to attain better economies of scale and become the world's dominant telecoms company in the "wired" world. The new giant may well have to provide bandwidth for free. Most of its money will be made from a myriad of new services, sold on the back of its global network.

It may be no surprise if they in turn gobble up a mature Cisco and Nortel and create NorCisc Services! Possibly the world's most valuable company! Impossible? Remember, in the wireless Internet, only the last 100 metres is "wireless." For Cisco and Nortel, much of their product business is complimentary but will fall prey to the "falling price boom" within five to ten years. Perhaps this union is not only possible but desirable in the long term!

Within the next few years,

they may become **the leading**

retailer in the world

way before the 2020s.

Nordicsson

Europe will have to unite not only as one market, but as one producer if it is to really capitalize on the new economy. The merger of a wounded Ericsson and a booming Nokia might create the most valuable company in Europe, and the world leader in the wireless Internet. Companies such as Symbian and Psion may well be pulled into its orbit as Europe gets its revenge in Round Two of the Internet Wars.

AmaWalmart

A dynamic meeting of minds, skills, and resources between the leading retailers of the online and offline worlds. Within the next few years, they may become the leading retailer in the world way before the 2020s – perhaps a company with more than 100 million repeat customers? The most powerful customer information base on the planet! And, each bit of information used to add value to the customer at each point of contact.

MicroGenome

Just as Microsoft made its fortune by providing software for computing, this new company will make its money by focussing on the software for living things... the DNA blueprints for life itself. This Microsoft of the Biotech Age will be the archetypal Information Age company, producing no physical products, but packaging and distributing knowledge in a way that will forever change our world – selling genetic blueprints to farmers, drug manufacturers and homes. Homes? How will the "gene machine" in your kitchen ever be able to make a lettuce atom-by-atom without the "blueprint" downloaded over the network from MicroGenome?

MicroGenome will be born from the scores of organizations now racing to map and patent the human genome. Of the companies currently working in this field, perhaps ten will survive. MicroGenome will have a monopoly on the software of living things, and will eventually be put under the same kind of anti-monopolistic pressure that Microsoft is today.

As global bandwidth increases, a big focus will be "delivery of content." That means music, movies, television, news and just about any other form of information and entertainment.

Energen

By 2020, ongoing consolidation will have left only one major global oil company in the Top Ten, and they will be a product of continued consolidation.

MitMitToy

The sole remaining Japanese company among the big players, a strategic fusion of such once-invincible giants as Mitsubishi, Mitsui, and Toyota. Japan missed out on the software boom because English is the universal language of the software industry. This will continue to restrict Japan's growth in the Information Age. The same will apply to China, whereas India will boom on the back of its English language skills. In 1989, Japanese companies represented 50 percent of world markets. Today that figure is 14 percent, and falling steadily. MitMitToy, just one possible acronym of some possible survivors, will represent Japanese interest in the world's Top Ten.

NanoIBM

IBM will retain a place in the Top Ten by investing aggressively in key new technologies. "Big Blue" already owns many patents in nanotechnology, giving it the edge in the radical new science of building microscopic machines atom by atom. As BioTech evolves to be an information industry, IBM is also likely to become a major player in this major new industry.

TimeWarnerDirect

As global bandwidth increases, a big focus will be "delivery of content." That means music, movies, television, news, and just about any other form of information and entertainment. In the not-too-distant future, TimeWarner will sell the bulk of their products directly to consumers over the Internet and will have to seek out alliances to open these flood gates. (Editor's note: this was written in August 1999, five full months before TimeWarner's groundbreaking merger with AOL.)

Financial services that are today only available to the wealthy will be available via the internet to anyone.

PersonalWealth.com

Financial services that are today only available to the wealthy will be available via the Internet to anyone. Software agents will provide instant real-time advice in increasingly complex and volatile markets. Any financial services players not totally geared to customized one-on-one services and advice will be Amazon'd by new players like PersonalWealth.com. Banks and other traditional financial services players that still think I'm ten people will succumb to this new customer-service paradigm.

Wireless Internet companies may well take over the mantle of retail banks as their networks provide the platforms for payments and transaction processing, and as their customer information becomes the most powerful value creator in their history.

General Electric

GE has such depth of management, and such a wide range of competencies, that we're willing to bet it will be able to adapt and reinvent itself to meet the demands of the New Economy. We'll even go as far as to say that GE will become the prime example of what many management experts regard as an oxymoron: a dynamic conglomerate.

Investing in the coming boom

It doesn't matter what we call these companies. Just take a look at the boom sectors for the new economy. They're all built around changing consumer preferences.

All the "old" players, from SAB and the mining groups to ONSL, will shed jobs dramatically. The only real job growth will be in the "new" boom industries.

In the industrial economy, say in the auto sector, your market share might creep up from 60 percent to 61 percent. In the new economy, say in software, your share could easily rocket from 40 percent to 90 percent. That's the kind of potential you want to invest in.

That's when you'll start catching sight of the real Blue Chips of the future, even though many of them won't be making profits for years to come. You'll have to ask yourself: What am I really interested in as an investor? Size, profits, or growth in market value? Think carefully. Act decisively. And remember...whatever you do, you'll be putting your trust and your money in the most volatile, most dynamic stock of them all: The Future!

7

Government and the economy

The power of positive chaos

"Always looking on the bright side, forever awaiting the dawn that breaks through the darkness, we are, by nature, a species encoded for optimism. All the more so when we cast our gaze to the near and not-so-near future."

Averting our eyes from the prospect of Apocalypse, we see glittering, celestial city-states, driven by the economics of desire – get what you want, whenever you want it – and free from the scourges of crime, poverty, and disease. We see vibrant democracies and markets overflowing with goods and entrepreneurial flair. We see the future, and it works. We see Utopia.

Originally conceived as the heart of an ideal republic by Sir Thomas More, the 16th century English humanist and statesman, the universal dream of Utopia has captured the imagination of everyone from Plato to Marx to H G Wells. But if you're looking for Utopia in the modern world, you might want to bear the origins of the word in mind. It springs from the Greek "Ou," meaning "not," and "topos," meaning "place."

In other words: the road to Utopia is the road to nowhere

Of course, this hasn't stopped philosophers, politicians, and billionaires from trying to bring their own visions of Utopia to life. You'll find a perfect example in New Utopia, a fantasy kingdom-in-the-making in the middle of the Caribbean. Presided over by a self-appointed monarch who calls himself

Even as we see

an **explosion** in

the number of countries,

the number of languages,

and currencies

will dwindle!

Prince Lazarus – in reality, an Oklahoma businessman named Howard Turney – New Utopia is being sold to the super-wealthy as a tax-free paradise where life is a constant carnival of shopping, gambling, ocean-cruising, and counting your money.

Financed by bonds and investments in New Utopia's fictitious currency, the grand scheme may turn out to be nothing more than a scam. Already, "Prince Lazarus" has fallen afoul of America's Securities and Exchange Commission, which put a freeze on his online transactions. For now, this New Utopia remains firmly grounded in the middle of nowhere.

Even so, the notion of small city-states, governed for and by the people who inhabit them, is not quite as far-fetched as it may seem. You might be forgiven for thinking, as telecommunications wraps the world in a digital skin, that there might be fewer borders, fewer countries and greater uniformity.

In fact, it appears that the opposite may be true.

Globalization and technology could enable ever-smaller countries to "go it alone." How about the independent state of Scotland? Or Wales? Or even New York? As we redefine the notion of what constitutes a "country," we could see a fractal-style explosion of new territories, independent and interdependent in a thriving, hotly-competitive networked trade zone.

By 2020, for example, India will be more populous than China. Its 28 states may well be able to redefine themselves as countries, even if the process leads to a series of bloody civil wars. But even as we see more countries, we will begin to see fewer currencies, with the US Dollar and the Euro eventually dominating world markets.

In the same way, English will become the dominant language of commerce. Although only 322 million people currently speak English as a first language, as opposed to 885 million for Mandarin, the scale swings dramatically to 1.5 billion when you include those who speak English as a second language.

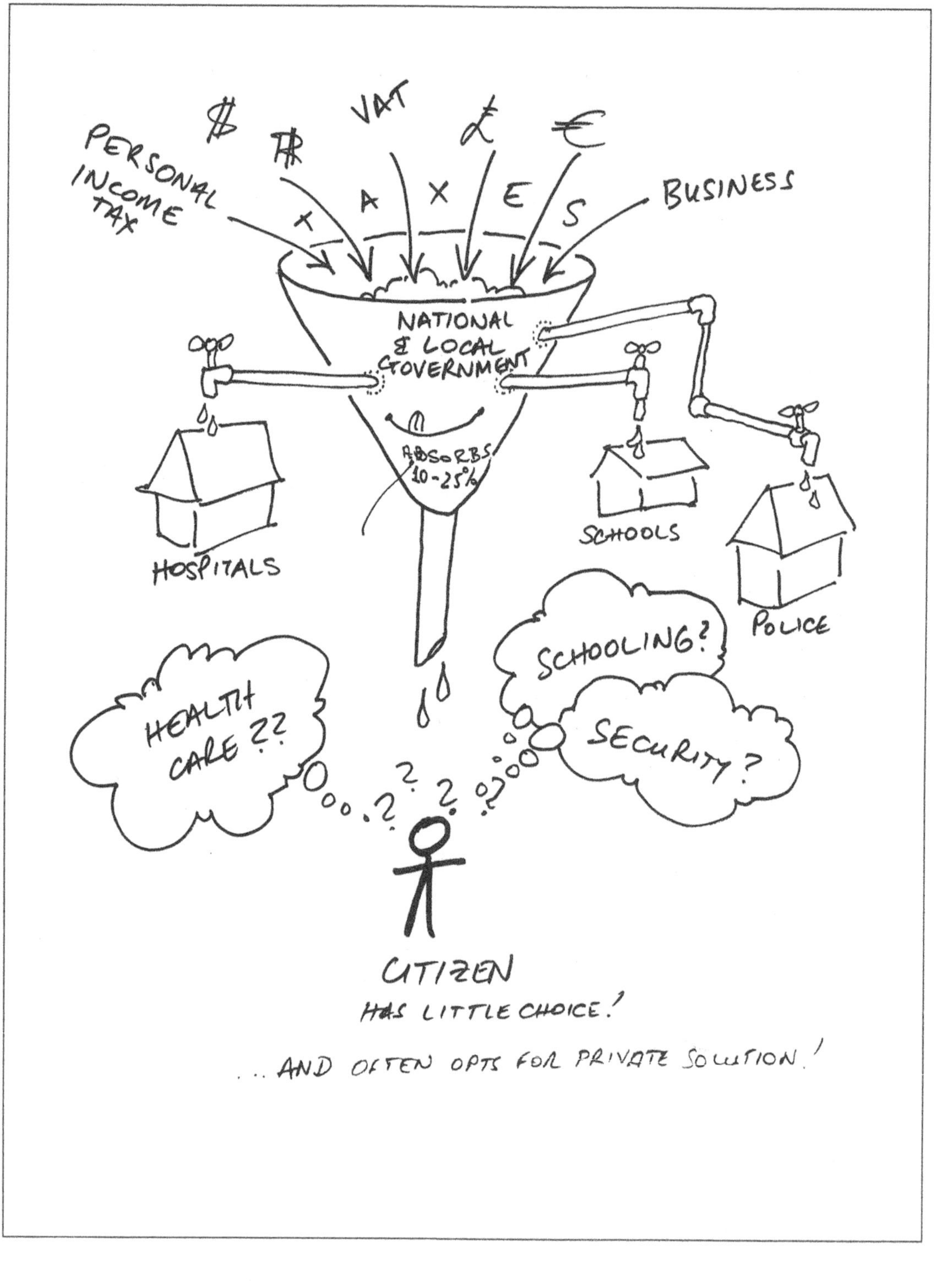

$ R £ € VAT
PERSONAL INCOME TAX
TAXES
BUSINESS
NATIONAL & LOCAL GOVERNMENT
ABSORBS 10–25%
HOSPITALS
SCHOOLS
POLICE
HEALTH CARE ??
SCHOOLING?
SECURITY?
CITIZEN
HAS LITTLE CHOICE!
... AND OFTEN OPTS FOR PRIVATE SOLUTION!

Let's hammer the message home again: Be literate! Speak English! Get wired!

It may not give you an instant ticket to Utopia, but it will give you the key to a better, smarter life in the destination that is common to all our dreams. The future.

Government of the future, by the future, for the future

In the now-declining Industrial Economy, governments have tended to "macro-manage" the economy as a way of increasing central control and protecting markets. But as we move into the New Bioeconomy, it's getting more and more important for politicians to shift their focus.

They've got to start thinking small.

They've got to learn to inspire rather than control.

New regulation should focus on creating a context for maximum economic opportunity, with easier access to education and increased free-market activity. In the global arena, governments will have to seek a new balance between the inbuilt desire to "control," and the need to "add value" in a fast-changing market.

To sum up...

A challenging context...

- An open global economy
- Transnational businesses
- Assets becoming more intangible (intellectual and electronic)
- A shrinking tax base

...demands a changing role for governments...

- Add value and don't do anything that can be done better by someone else, e.g. security, health care and education
- Get more efficient and smaller
- Don't support any one side (e.g. trade unions, universities)

How does your government stack up?

– Create context for growth and social mores, e.g. drug control
– Fight new world wars, to win new skills and talents

...and an open global culture!

– Make people smarter
– Turn technophobia into techno-lust

Is anyone listening? It's easy to complain about close-minded, out-of-touch, backward-thinking politicians. It's easy to abandon hope and assume that governments are inherently incapable of getting it right. It's a lot harder to cut through the rhetoric, and propose solutions that might make a difference, now and in the future.

Here's my contribution to the debate.

Let's see how *your* government stacks up against these recommendations to create a context for maximum economic performance in the New Economy.

Sure, *your* government may already score highly on some of the points, but what else needs to be done? And, how much time do you have? How powerful will your economic tsunami be?

Do you have the kind of government and the attitudes necessary to surf the tsunami? How can your nation capitalize on the massive opportunities that an economic tsunami creates?

It's an open world
where real market power
has moved to the individual
consumer and investor.

An open letter to world governments

Ten things governments should do to surf the new economy tsunami!

Dear World Leader

While you're focussing on the traditional stuff of politics... here are a few bold things for your agenda that will put the people of your country first – before political priorities!

Here are a few things that might just turn the economy head-on to the new economic tsunami, create appropriate skills, make you a magnet for investment and thrive in radical new ways!

The world has changed. But then you know that. You speak about it often.

It's an open world where the real market power has moved from governments and large corporations to the "sovereign individual." As individuals and consumers, we have never had such personal power to shape markets and economies. In world markets, volatility is endemic but growth opportunities are everywhere. We all have a chance to make it in the global market – but only if we want to, and only if we consciously choose a relevant radical future! We need your help and leadership to create an increasingly competitive market environment that will enable us to thrive.

Here then are "Ten Things" that your government should consider doing immediately to create the environment for growth and wealth creation.

Own up to

the growth catalysts and

competitive

dynamics of

the new global economy!

1. **Own up!** We must own up to the growth catalysts and the competitive dynamics of the new global economy, even if these are not politically correct. Tell people that the "old" jobs are gone forever, that unemployment will increase before it can decline and that there are some new rules of work and wealth out there. What we need is intellectual honesty! You fully understand the realities of this global economy. It may be naive to believe that a politician can get off the political agenda for a while, but if you can and put the real needs of individuals first, then you will be remembered by history as the one who fulfilled community needs by capitalizing on the power of individuals. Communication is everything, people can understand the economic issues facing us if we take the effort to communicate properly. Given the same open information about the present, my experience is that people across a wide front will come to the same conclusions about the future. But it may initially not be politically correct – this will take great political courage, and strategic patience!
2. **Create the skills for the 21st century economy!** There's no shortage of work or opportunity in the world – only a shortage of skills and ideas! The trouble is that the skills that will fuel the new economy are not based on muscle power but on the ability to harness the power of the mind. We need thinking skills, fundamentally different knowledge and service skills. Let's stop trying to protect the old jobs – these jobs are gone forever – and let's start creating the skills that will fuel future jobs. Skill creation is a much longer process than job creation (or job protection!) but the only one that will bring lasting social and economic benefits.
3. **Fast track people to become economically relevant**. Give people a basic context in which they can grow – they need to:

   Be literate. Let's focus on the immediately relevant skills. Basic literacy may no longer be an issue in your country, but what about economic literacy? What about entrepreneurial literacy? Apart from basic literacy, that's what is needed to create economic sparks! In this economy, basic literacy includes the knowledge of where the jobs are, and where they are not; what skills are relevant and which are dead-end.

Germany is changing age-old cultures

by fast-tracking people

to become

economically relevant!

Speak English. Apart from the people who speak English as their first language, already more than 1 billion people worldwide speak English as a second language. The language war has been won – put aside national language priorities – get on the economic fast track.

Get wired. Let's drive for universal Internet access in schools, libraries and public places. We already have a great telecommunications infrastructure, now let's open it up for everyone. Get every corporation to make their infrastructure available for this purpose, even if only after hours!

4. **We need new attitudes to work, jobs and the concepts of employment.** Even Germany has embarked on a six-point campaign to change personal attitudes to innovation and entrepreneurship:

   - **Go for it – be enterprising!** The new economy offers an abundance of opportunities. All it takes is initiative and entrepreneurial spirit! Everybody can be an entrepreneur!
   - **Think of it – innovate!** Competition forces you to keep innovating! Entrepreneurs strive to improve on what they make and how they make it! We need innovative entrepreneurs!
   - **Let them do it – deregulate!** Government is regulating business activities, often with good intentions but with damaging side effects. Government should set goals but let companies decide on their own how to achieve these goals!
   - **Be nimble – be flexible and adapt!** In a time of rapid change, business must adapt quickly. Nimble workers who never stop learning will succeed!
   - **Better by far – globalize!** Information technology allows people to work together even when separated by vast distances. Decentralization gives people more flexibility and greater responsibility. Entrepreneurs thrive on decentralization.
   - **Save for your future – make pensions sustainable!** In our pension system the young support the old. Today we all live longer and have fewer children. To sustain the pension system we must have private savings. Germany is striving to change age-old attitudes to entrepreneurship and personal success.

The digital skin is

the highway of the new economy –

let's remove all constraints to

free access!

5. **Let's invest radically in education – pay teachers amazing salaries.** I should want to become a teacher for the money, rather than choose to be a business executive! That's the way to attract the best teachers into the profession. Isn't that what we all want for our children?

6. **Remove central (government) control of the education system!** You can't have centralized development of skills in a decentralized economy. By all means let government allocate a portion of its tax revenues to education – just don't give it directly to schools! Let government give "education vouchers" to parents, so that they can "spend" them at a school of their choice. Let's create market forces in schools – only those schools that guarantee employment/jobs/work will survive! Wouldn't you send your child to a school that guaranteed a job on graduation? Education companies in the IT industry have been doing that for years! Create the kind of skills that have relevance in the new economy. Create community fever for the new skills/jobs – it's really OK to be self-employed, it's OK to work in a service industry like tourism, it's OK to be a web designer/programmer rather than a doctor or lawyer – these are the new professions!

7. **Create the telecommunications infrastructure for the information economy!** If it is not already totally deregulated, deregulate the telecommunications industry now! This is the highway infrastructure for the new economy – we must have the best and everyone must have access. In Germany, deregulation in telecommunications created 40,000 net new jobs in the first year! It's the same wherever you look. Let real competition into all sectors of the telecommunications market, to create real growth and real new jobs.

   Once you've deregulated the market, then break up the major infrastructure owners into two companies – one focussed on infrastructure and the other focussed on services. Let everyone have unlimited access to the infrastructure. "They" don't own the infrastructure, we do! Let anyone who wants to deliver video-on-demand or any other new services over the old copper cable infrastructure! Open up the networks and maximize economic opportunity for all.

8. **Incentivize investment in "The Right Stuff"!** Stop providing tax and other incentives for the acquisition of Industrial Age capital goods (e.g. automobiles) and focus instead on Information Age "stuff" that will build skills and can create economic advantage! There should, for example, be no VAT

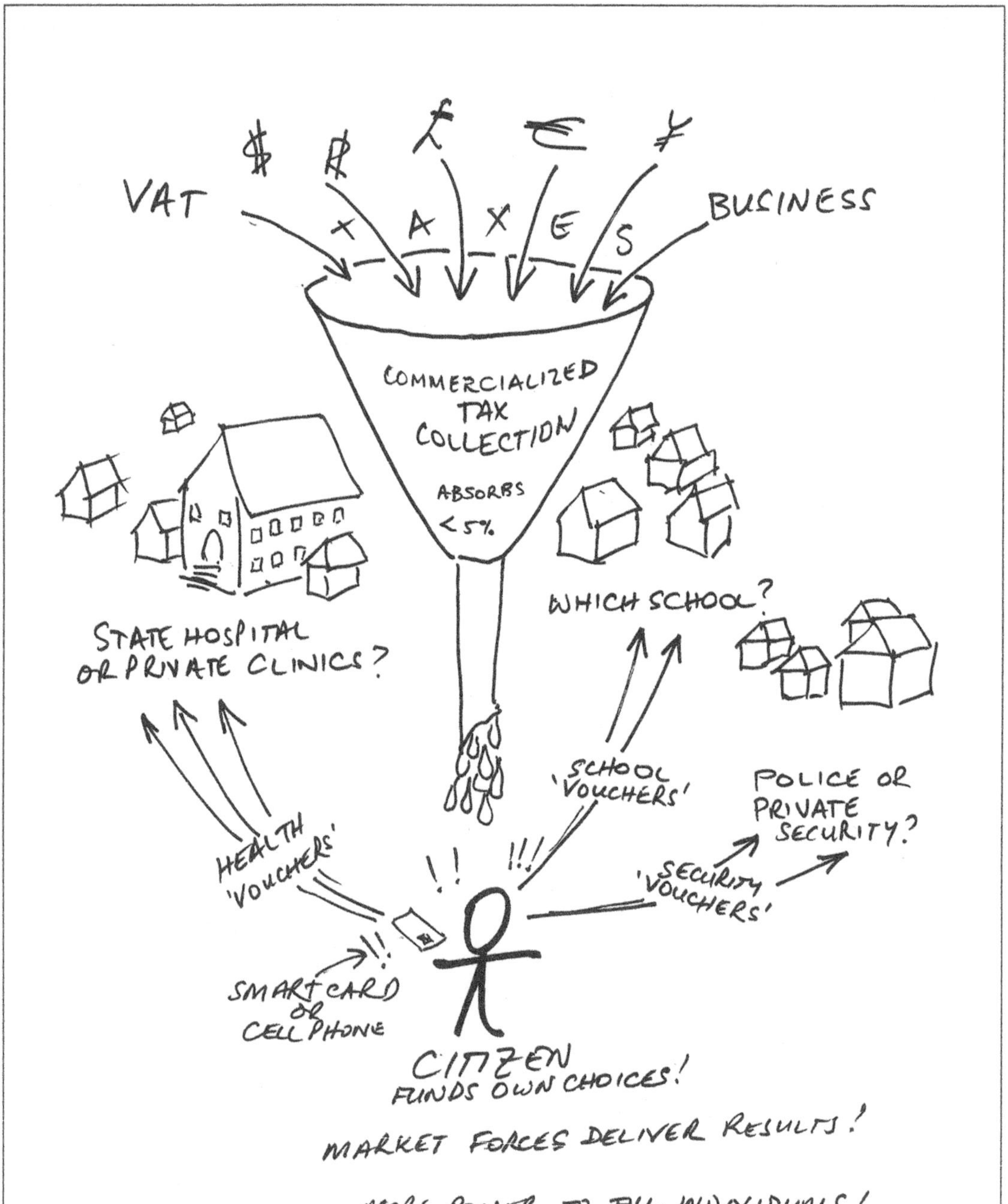
VAT
$ R £ € ¥
T A X E S
BUSINESS
COMMERCIALIZED TAX COLLECTION
ABSORBS <5%
STATE HOSPITAL OR PRIVATE CLINICS?
WHICH SCHOOL?
'SCHOOL VOUCHERS'
POLICE OR PRIVATE SECURITY?
HEALTH 'VOUCHERS'
'SECURITY VOUCHERS'
!! !!!
SMART CARD OR CELL PHONE
CITIZEN
FUNDS OWN CHOICES!
MARKET FORCES DELIVER RESULTS!
MORE POWER TO ALL INDIVIDUALS!

on computers, software, communication charges and Internet access! There should be direct personal tax incentives for the acquisition of such Information Age goods, services and infrastructure.

9. **Attract global skills!** Create an environment in which they will want to work. The world's best skills are attracted to the world's most exciting projects. Apart from the obvious (a crime-free, gun-free environment, etc.) you need low taxes and investment by the world's leading companies. Your country needs to become the most desirable place to start new venture capital businesses. Point 9 below ought to help!

10. **Lower corporate taxes and get rid of personal income tax!** Any individual or business offering services based on services, intellectual capital and ideas (rather than the trade in physical goods) is already able to move royalties, revenues and profits seamlessly around the world – much of it slipping through the traditional income tax net! Today, it is sometimes difficult to tell whether someone is actually "working" or not! As service and information work increases to more than 50 percent of GDP (OECD figures are now already there), income tax becomes increasingly difficult and expensive to collect. Let's get rid of personal income tax and replace it with a consumption tax (a super-VAT). VAT has already proven to be far cheaper to collect than income tax. Let's do it now and take the ceiling off wealth creation and job creation!

11. **Create an inspirational economic policy!** This must be an economic policy that every businessperson can explain and understand. In terms of economic strategy, let's be a little crazy – but not stupid! Capture the imagination of the world's investors and investment analysts. Be different, be noticed! Be the place to invest and work! Be the best at attracting the new Information Age businesses, new jobs and new skills.

Right, World Leader, when you've done this you can get back to winning the next election – or perhaps put your feet up after a job well done!
Yours passionately,

Wolfgang Grulke
CEO FutureWorld

HOW IS MY GOVERNMENT DOING SO FAR?

SCORE = ✓

	POOR!	OK!	GREAT!!
1. OWNING UP TO THE GROWTH CATALYSTS & COMPETITIVE DYNAMICS OF NEW ECONOMY			
2. CREATING THE SKILLS FOR THE NEW ECONOMY			
3. FAST TRACKING PEOPLE TO BECOME ECONOMICALLY RELEVANT			
4. INVESTING RADICALLY IN EDUCATION			
5. REMOVING CENTRAL CONTROL FROM EDUCATION – MAKING IT MARKET-DRIVEN			
6. CREATING THE TELECOMMUNICATIONS INFRASTRUCTURE FOR THE NEW ECONOMY			
7. INCENTIVIZING INVESTMENT IN "THE RIGHT STUFF"			
8. ATTRACTING GLOBAL SKILLS			
9. LOWERING CORPORATE TAXES AND ABOLISHING PERSONAL TAX			
10. CREATING AN INSPIRATIONAL ECONOMIC POLICY			

ANY NATION WITH LESS THAN 5 TICKS UNDER "GREAT" IS MOST LIKELY NOT GOING TO BE GLOBALLY COMPETITIVE!

So, how is your government doing so far? You may get a better idea by completing the questionnaire opposite. See how it rates out of a total score of 50 (which equates to heaven on earth!).

The aftermath

Is this Open Letter just a way of shooting arrows into the political darkness?

Why not create some spontaneous combustion.

Why not turn the tax authorities from the role of economic police force into a powerful driver of your country's future economic success. They could be the *gearbox* of the economy – for efficient tax collection and for the distribution of funds (via vouchers) for schooling, health and security to individuals at large. Much of it would obviously have to be done using the electronic tools of the new economy – the Internet, smart cards and cellphones.

For vouchers read "value." These would not be paper vouchers but value allocated and distributed either via smart cards or stored on cellphones. Individuals could then exchange this value simply by swiping the card or calling a designated number at approved points (schools, doctors, security companies, etc).

If successful, the tax authority might even be listed on the stock exchange in future.

They would be a highly desirable e-commerce hub providing more than just taxation services, to the public and private sector. Eventually they would have to tender openly for the government's taxation business! Now that would prove them to be a real value-added business in the true spirit of free markets. And everyone would benefit.

What if senior representatives from the police force considered the impact of the power of the consumer on their business: "Why just have 'vouchers' for education? Why not give everyone Security Vouchers instead of funding the police directly?" Interesting! This would enable the police in your neighborhood to compete with private security companies for your funds! This would sort out the arguments about quality of service within months, community by community.

Imagine a market-driven,
customer-centric police force!

We have to find **radical economic strategies** that will catapult us on a **fast track** into the economy of the future. We **can't do this** by **repeating** the economic **experience of the past.** We have to **learn from the future.**

In any event, many police stations already have "panic buttons" – connected to private security firms. Whatever you choose to call it, the privatization of the police force has already begun!

So, "vouchers" not just for schooling, but also for health care and security. Everyone, employed or unemployed, would receive them and could spend them with the organization of their choice.

Putting the power firmly into the hands of the individual.
Putting real market forces into central and local government!
Capitalizing on the power of positive chaos!

Will your government do something quite as "radical" as these recommendations imply? Unlikely – the political risks are too great and require somewhat radical leadership, not unlike that provided by Margaret Thatcher in the UK in the 1970s. Your politicians may just be too good at understanding the political implications to take such a radical (and risky) path.

However, it is my sincere belief that today, the path to economic success cannot be turned incrementally.

Increasingly, we have to find radical economic strategies that will catapult us on a fast track into the economy of the future. We can't do this by repeating the economic experience of the past. We have to learn from the future.

Successful governments will be those who can leverage the new power of the individual and create a context in which communities of individuals can thrive.
As individuals we know we have it within us.
Our governments must believe that they can lead world economic thinking in the art of the possible.

8

Ten lessons from the future

You are what you do!

With perfect 20/20 hindsight, looking back from the year 2020, we may recall that the turn of the millennium represented the realization of the age of the individual – the start of true fractal economics.

Openness and technology were the catalysts, but the culture change had its roots in Woodstock.

Do you remember the 1970s?

- The dawning of the Age of Aquarius, Peace and Love
- The birth of the culture of the individual
- The start of a major world recession and the advent of the Japanese Miracle

Do you remember the 1990s?

- The rise of a global economy based on true free-market principles
- The domination of world markets by the United States
- The emergence of a new spirit of peace and democracy, alongside a proliferation of ethnic conflicts

From our
perspective in 2020,
what will we
have learned?

Do you remember "The Millennium"?

Cast your mind forward to the year 2020. You are there. Choose a specific date. Now, from your "future perfect" perspective, look back to the turn of the millennium. And try to remember...

Where were you when the clock struck midnight? What were you doing? What do you recall?

- Ethnic conflicts and AIDS
- Widespread disillusionment with government
- The end of heroes, and the rise of human politicians
- Businesses that are more powerful than governments
- Pop stars becoming part of the mainstream corporate environment
- The rise and rise of individual rights, consumerism and investor power
- The icon of the 1960s, "The Pill," giving way to the icon of the 1990s, "The Bill" (of Rights)
- The end of nationalism, and an explosion of new loyalties

From our perspective in 2020, what will we have learned? If we had known in 2000 what we will know in 2020, how would that have changed our way of thinking? Our attitudes? Our actions? What are the new "rules of the game"?

What are the lessons we can learn from the future?

In the course of our journey from the start of the 1970s to the end of the 2020s, it will have become apparent that some things cannot be learned through rigorous analysis alone.

To fully understand the lessons of perfect 20/20 Hindsight and 2020 Vision, you have to take a big step backwards and focus on the macro implications of the future.

It's like looking at a swarm of bees – you cannot determine their purpose by analyzing a bee molecule by molecule. The purpose of the swarm emerges only when you step backwards and take a look at the big picture.

In the same way, the Ten Lessons from the Future are "emergent properties" of the 60-year time span we have considered.

The *effect* of the Ten Lessons from the Future can however be much more short-term. They should be translated into strategic actions, for your business, for yourself, your family or your investments. Strategic actions that you take *today* – to shape your future in the long term.

Here then

are my

10 lessons

from the future!

1 Information and ideas fuel the new global economy!

Pure knowledge is worthless. Skills and ideas are everything.

It may seem strange that a "knowledge economy" places so little economic value on knowledge. If you don't believe me, consider the average academic and what he or she earns. It's only when we turn knowledge into skills – skills for which the market is prepared to pay – that true economic value is created.

So, while the new economy can truly be called an "economy of plenty," thanks to the plethora of choices for consumers and investors, and the unprecedented ease of access to information, the truth is that plenty is sometimes just not enough. We're drowning in knowledge and information, but we're starved for skills. It's not *what you know* any more. It's *what you do* with what you know that really makes the difference.

2 Biotechnology is the second information revolution!

Information professionals, rather than biologists, are creating an economy that will have a more profound impact on our world than anything seen in the Digital Age.

Just as computers have operating systems and application software to make them functional, so does every living organism – plant, human, animal – come equipped with its own special brand of software called DNA. The rapidly developing science of biotechnology seeks to manage the complexity of the more than 3 billion bits of information in each DNA molecule. In the race to break through the barriers of genetic engineering, it is information professionals and information companies that are leading the way.

Once biotechnology products enter world markets on a broad scale, it's quite likely that the economic impact will outstrip the scale and pace of the Information Economy itself. We may well realize that the Information Economy was nothing more than Phase One of the Bioeconomy, completing the transition from a "tangible" economy to one in which "intangibles" have the real value... where incredibly *small and complex* technologies replace the *big and simple* technologies of the Industrial Economy.

3 It's the "personal" age!

As the focus of the new economy shifts from centralized control to individual responsibility, everything from computing to healthcare to manufacturing to energy production will feel the benefits of decentralization.

Never in the history of humanity has the individual had so much personal power, and so much freedom to choose.

Thanks to affordable home computers and the Internet, individuals can now equip themselves with the kind of reach, power, and influence previously reserved for large corporations. In another sense and context, "power" is being reclaimed from national utility companies as personal turbines give domestic consumers an undreamed-of independence from the electricity grid. On the healthcare front, networks of small community clinics, linked into the "digital skin" of the Internet, will increasingly take the place of overcrowded, under-resourced state hospitals.

Think "small" and personal – and look for network effects to create maximum resonance and growth.

4 Leadership can be widely shared!

Organizations are beginning to resemble flocks of birds, as individuals take turns to determine direction and lead aspects of the enterprise.

The long-term consequences of personal empowerment and the rise of "learning organizations" are proving difficult for many Industrial Age managers to accept. As organizations become more and more fractal in nature, the need for old-style management diminishes, even as there is a desperate need for leadership. Management jobs will decrease significantly as the nature of the hierarchy changes. Managers will have to let go and let younger employees lead aspects of the business.

The need for a shared vision and purpose is paramount, as organizations evolve into complex, dynamic entities that draw their inspiration from the positive chaos of the natural world.

Leadership will be an essential quality at all levels of an organization, for all individuals.

5 Fractal/non-linear behavior is the norm!

Don't be afraid of chaos. It's just biological behavior.

Wherever you look in the new economy, you see the same kinds of fractal characteristics. Understand the new rules, and you'll realize that chaos is not something to fear or resist. It's just biology in action.

In a world governed by "Butterfly Effects" and "Bifurcation Points," it's no good trying to build your future on the successes of your past. Don't be afraid to be intuitive. The worst thing you can do is nothing.

The organizations of the Industrial Age went out of their way to avoid risk; the organizations of the new economy go out of their way to embrace it. Companies that live and work on the "edge of chaos" have a way of making people want to do business with them. They're exciting, resonant, dynamic. Taking risks is safer than doing nothing. Build an organizational spirit that encourages it.

6 The "unknown" is the realm of all possibilities!

Uncertainty presents a moment of real freedom. Leave the baggage of experience behind. Take a giant leap into the Great Unknown.

To experience true freedom, you have to let go of the past. You have to empty your mind of the baggage of experience, and stride with head held high into the realm of uncertainty.

This line of thinking, common in Eastern spirituality, gives us an excellent mechanism for coping with the volatility and chaos of our everyday lives. In the new economy, the worst thing that can happen is that every day of your future is mapped out, every new step planned and modeled on what worked in the past.

Certainty leaves little room for innovation and personal freedom. Open your mind to new possibilities. Embrace the unknown. Make the future happen.

7 Eat yourself – become your own worst nightmare!

Don't wait for new competitors to show you how customers ought to be serviced. Do it yourself, while you can still afford it.

You will never out-think the young new competitors riding in your slipstream, unless you are prepared to cannibalize yourself.

Even the brightest, boldest new companies can turn into monstrous bureaucracies if they believe too strongly in the propaganda of their own success. They, too, have to learn to "eat themselves" as each new disruptive technology comes along.

The worst time to act is when you no longer have a choice and your options are limited. Act while you can, and you still have the money to fund the transition.

8 You can no longer learn just from experience!

The faster things change, the less relevant experience becomes. You must learn from the future.

Experience has high value in a stable, unchanging market, where the dynamics of competition change slowly. Today's global markets are the exact antithesis of this. There are no precedents for the dramatic changes that are shaping the business environment of the 21st century. The rules we need to understand new markets have not been written yet. Learning from experience alone is no longer an option.

In order to thrive in the new world economy, we will have to learn from the future. What are the consumer lifestyles of the future? What are the regulatory norms of the future? How can we design our businesses to succeed in the future?

It's no use simply extrapolating from what we know and where we are today. That kind of thinking almost always leads to the wrong conclusions.

9 Don't compete!

We're living in the most competitive market in history. So don't compete! Find white-space opportunities in which you have no competitors.

Establishing a strong market presence in new, innovative markets is by far the cheapest way of gaining market share.

The win–lose model applies particularly in the second half of industry cycles, where there is massive competition based on price.

The win–win model grows the market overall, and establishes brand new high-growth markets.

That's where we'd all choose to be – and now you have that choice!

MY OWN
TEN LESSONS
FOR MY FUTURE?

10 It's one world, one mind, one time!

Our planet is wrapped in a digital skin, uniting all people, with one internal clock that runs 24 × 7 × 52. Use the entire global resource base. Beat to your customers' drum.

The new global economy is not just about open, global markets. It's about global resources: about sourcing the best raw materials, products, and even people, without having to worry about the once-intimidating constraints of national borders, boundaries, and time-zones.

Above all, it's about the fact that anyone, anywhere is potentially your customer. As exciting as this is, it puts a series of profound new pressures on your business and customer service. You can't hide behind weekends, working hours or public holidays anymore. Customer expectations are almost impossible to meet without automated processes that ensure your business is open 24 × 7 × 52.

The advent of the fax machine turned up our internal clocks, so that anything that took longer than a day was considered unacceptable. E-commerce turns the screws some more. It truly is the "I want it and I want it NOW!" culture.

Instant response, while you hold your breath, is becoming the norm, not the exception. This is the pulse of your customers' expectations – beat to this, or perish.

We stand at the cusp of a new age,
filled with massive opportunities for
business and personal growth.

Whoever understands the new rules – my Ten Lessons from the Future – and acts on them *today*, will rule the competitive jungle of tomorrow. Will that person be you?

You must decide.

But two things are for sure.

The future is the place where you are destined
to spend most of the rest of your life.

And you'll never get out of it alive.

For the first time in history, whoever and wherever you are,
your future is a matter of choice, not chance.

So choose wisely. Act now, while you still have the luxury of choice.

With a tsunami on its way, taking risks is safer than doing nothing!
Learn the lessons of tomorrow, today.
The future belongs to you!

Appendix

The information age scorecard

"The Information Age Scorecard is a unique Internet-based tool that will enable you, as a business leader, to see how prepared your company is for the future. Just how ready are you to compete against the new Information Age companies that are radically reshaping the rules of business, competitiveness and your industry?

This questionnaire will probe your perceptions of your company's current reality and your views of how your company ought to be positioned in future. FutureWorld's Ten Business Commandments – the business imperatives for the Information Economy (also described at www.futureworld.co.za) are used as a basis for structuring the questions and the analysis in the Information Age Scorecard.

Once you have completed the questionnaire, you will be given an analysis of your ratings.

Finally, you will be able to compare your own perceptions against those of your peers in other companies around the world, both in your own specific industry, and overall.

Clearly the quality of the database will improve over time as more and more organizations participate. You will be able to come back in future, to see how you compare against a wider sample of participants.

Here is a sample of a typical questionnaire page:

THE INFORMATION AGE SCORECARD

Statement 1a: We treat the world as our market

		1	2	3	4	5	6	7	8	9	10	
Is this relevant to your business?	*irrelevant*	○	○	○	○	○	○	●	○	○	○	*very relevant*
The statement describes the CURRENT REALITY in your business	*totally disagree*	○	○	○	●	○	○	○	○	○	○	*totally agree*
This is where your business SHOULD be in the future	*totally disagree*	○	○	○	○	○	○	○	○	●	○	*totally agree*
This is where your business WILL be in the future	*totally disagree*	○	○	○	○	○	○	●	○	○	○	*totally agree*

In order to assess how your organization rates you will be asked to score your organization against 48 statements (like the sample above) describing the "ideal" Information Age business. Each rating can be scored between 1 and 10. In each statement you will be asked the following questions.

1. How relevant is this statement to your business?
2. How do you rate your current reality against this ideal state? (The Current Reality)
3. Where do you believe your business SHOULD be in the future? (The Ideal Future)
4. Where do you believe your business WILL be in the future? (The Likely Future)

You can choose an appropriate date in the next five years or so as your time horizon. The difference between 2 and 3 above will give an indication of the degree of change that you believe is required (we call this the *Change Index*).

The difference between 3 and 4 will give us an indication how ready the organization is to implement the changes you believe are required (we call this the *Competency Index*). Both indices are weighted by the relevance you attach to the statement.

Based on your scores we will identify the key areas for change and competency development.

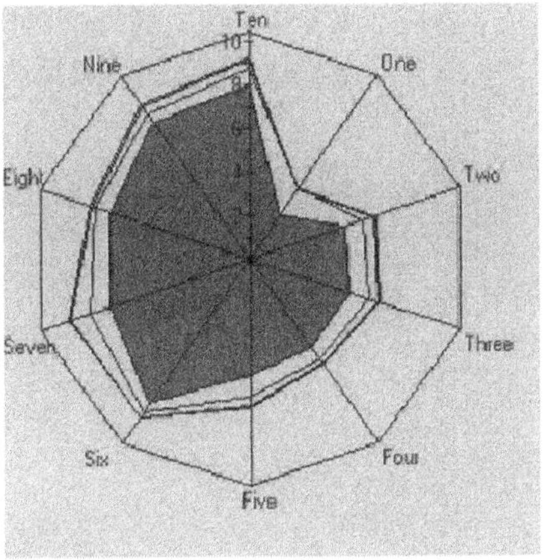

Once you have completed the scorecard you will be presented with a radar chart summarizing your responses, highlighting areas of perceived strengths and weaknesses against each of the Ten Business Commandments.

The centre area shows your perception of your business's "Current Reality", the next ring shows your perception of the "Likely Future" and the outer ring shows your perception of the "Desired Future."

You will also be able to compare your rankings with others who have participated in the Information Age Scorecard.

To start the process...

1. Go to www.futureworld.org
2. Select "Information Age Scorecard" from the menu
3. Follow the instructions to complete the Scorecard as an Individual User

So what about *your* future?